DEACTIVATING THE CODE OF FAILURE

Pinky Thompson

Deactivating the Code of Failure

ISBN 978-0-620-82536-8

First published in South Africa in 2020 by Pinky Thompson.

ACKNOWLEDGMENT

I thank God, Almighty. My heart is full of praise for He kept me, redeemed me, and He, the giver of life deemed it fit to unleash a new lease on life for me that glorifies His Holy name.

My deepest gratitude goes to the best mom, my rock, Mrs. Mohlapa Magdelina Selepe, who raised me and my two lovely sisters with unwavering strength and love. After the passing of my father, Mr. Elias Mamokwanta Selepe; my mom had to summon courage in the midst of grief. During her mourning phase, she hastily had to adjust herself to her newfound reality of widowhood. Such harsh reality propelled her to pack away her tears and step into her new role as a single parenting mom. She stood in the gap and fitted well in my father's boots. She did it with so much love, grace and devotion inspiring us to be the best version of ourselves.

We were her little, pretty good girls. She never wished for us to let the world change who we were. Every day, I wore my best manners and studied diligently just to hear my mom say, "Good girl!" For me, that was it, a "Code" that moulded and kept me grounded through the years. Today, I am a loving and devoted mother to my brilliant and handsome son, Tshireletso and ours is a fantastic journey, and our love runs deep and pure. To all the servants of God, family, and friends, your prayers were never in vain. You stood with me, celebrated my victories and lifted me countless times during trials. You embraced me and navigated me through the righteous path applying your adept concept. You are, and always will be, beacons in my life.

CONTENTS

INTRODUCTION

This book will take you through the inner world and the turbulent journey of Megan, a 23-year-old woman whose story is both heart-breaking and inspiring. It sheds light on her lived experience, in terms of her fears, adversities and moral values learned, as well as her evolving beliefs about life. Despite the weight of all she has endured, Megan has developed a thick skin and a sensible outlook on life. Her analytical mind and approach allows her to navigate life's diverse and complex situations with grace and insight.

Megan had a narrow escape out of the effect of her bad and harrowing upbringing while growing up. Her early life was marked by chaos and emotional turmoil, leading her into deep depression and repeated suicide attempts. Yet, through sheer will and courage, she survived. That survival became her catalyst: Megan felt propelled and decided to take a stand to speak out and raise awareness. She began educating and collaborating with other young people, parents, and society to dismantle the familiar vicious cycles that have, for generations, obliterated and brought the youth and many families to their knees. She has sworn never to stop until her purpose is realised.

Through unwavering resilience and fortitude, Megan deactivated every code of failure in her life and vowed never to give up. She refused to be defined by failure. She became fiercely committed to conquer every obstacle that had once ruined her life, wounded her loved ones, and silenced her peers by transforming each scar into a testament of strength and renewal.

Some of the predicaments many had suffered during their childhood persisted into adulthood, leaving lasting scars, if not living the consequences already.

Megan anticipated that decoding the horrific experiences of the past could be a daunting and traumatic exercise for most of the youth to attempt. It required an accurate and compassionate approach. With conviction, she pledged to coach and support the youth in identifying their setbacks, dismantling their personal "codes" of failure, and decoding their past. Her mission was to empower them to accept, confront, and transcend their past failures, embracing a more liberated, fruitful, and richly fulfilling life.

Chapter 1

Upbringing

Megan was a typical township girl in her youth, an introvert brimming with life and dreams, one of which was to become a psychotherapist. She grew up in a dysfunctional family whereby, as it is in this era, it has become a norm to come from a family of single parenting without a proper family support base. This reality is no longer confined to race or geography but has emerged as a global dilemma; so widespread such that one could be forgiven for thinking that it's acceptable by society.

Our upbringing shapes us profoundly and plays a vital role in life, for better or worse. As children grow, conflict often arises when they begin to voice their opinions, express their desires, and assert their preferences. Yet, children are rarely granted a meaningful say in matters concerning their own welfare.

Children are often perceived purely as immature, neither expected to prescribe their own upbringing to their parents nor encouraged to articulate what they need or how they prefer to be raised. Their voices, though valid, are too often silenced, leaving them powerless to help the situation. Parents frequently make decisions without engaging their young ones. They disregard their children's feelings and opinions. Like any other child, Megan perceived her parents as heroes. She believed wholeheartedly that no one on earth was better than her folks. However, sooner than later, life unfolded. Megan came to realise that some of the choices her parents made were not only life-changing but also deeply misguided.

Taking you down the memory lane: how many times have you heard yourself or other parents say to a child: "Don't argue with me. Just get it done already. I'm your mother/father; you'll do as I say!" Before you can answer, pause for a moment. In all honesty, can you live with some of the decisions you once imposed on your children? As parents, every word we speak and every lesson we teach eventually catches up with us. These choices don't vanish with time; they echo. It may not be today, but it will surely resurface to haunt or elevate us in the near future. They always find their way back.

Children who had committed crimes continue to congest prisons to this day. Often, the root of their actions lies in misguided decisions, harmful pieces of advice, and lessons absorbed from their parents during their formative years. Over time, these influences shaped unruly behaviours that eventually led to law infringement. Now these children faces prosecution and imprisonment for choices that were, in part, moulded by their upbringing. The sad part is this: it's the children who face the music, while you, the parent, remain in the comfort of your home, perhaps shedding tears, losing sleep, or even distancing yourself from your child, calling them names and disowning them. But the truth of the matter is, neither your tears nor your anger will benefit your child in any way to escape the situation at hand.

Our children are vulnerable and many are in distress. Some feel like lost causes, while others have tragically died due to poor parental skills. Our children are faced with a multitude of challenges shaped by their diversified and unique complex circumstances. And in the midst of it all, they may not confide in us. But trust me, some children know what they know. They know who the instigator is. They know and recognize some of the chaos they are navigating; you as a parent had a hand in it, yet they are the ones bearing the consequences.

Food for thought: during my research, I encountered a troubling pattern. Most of the incarcerated children were adamant and firmly believed they were innocent. Blatantly so, without mincing their words, they declared that *the court of law had gotten it all wrong!* "Our parents are the guilty ones." They pointed to their upbringing; not as an excuse, but as the root cause. Your child is a jailbird today, convicted because of an ill-mannered behavioural issues that were disregarded or even encouraged during their foundational phase.

You have never reprimanded your child for fighting other children. Moreover, when they came home crying, you smacked them for not physically defending themselves. You didn't comfort them. You literally threatened them. You said: "if you ever come back home crying because someone beat you up, I will kill you myself. Don't even bother coming back to this house if you are to become such a coward." Dear parents, let's pause here. Let me break it down for you: through fear and aggression we have instilled in our children, many of us have unknowingly created our own monsters. In their desperation not to upset us, and out of fear of punishment, rejection, being homeless or being killed by you; poor kids resorted to fighting over trivial matters that came their way, simply to survive emotionally.

Children are sacred gifts, entrusted to our care by God. Every child grow up believing that their parents always have their best interests at heart and that every decision made is for their good. To them, we are the ultimate authority; wise, loving, and incapable of being wrong, so they think.

Parents must lead by example. When you lead by a good example, you teach your children without telling them what to do and demonstrating to them how it is done. Children rarely do what we say; they do what we do. When we lead with integrity, kindness, and consistency, we teach without preaching. "Thou I shall not be crucified," But too often, the opposite happens with our mommies and daddies. Naturally, parents tell their children not to lie, well and good. Yet down the line, those same children would later witness that their parents are the masters of double standards and deception, frighteningly two-faced and bending the truth. They see us doing the very same things we had advised them against. And in those moments, trust begins to crack. Let us not be the ones who crucify our children with contradictions. Instead, let us be the ones who guide them with grace, humility, and truth.

Consider this scenario: A well-learned father, a professed Christian for that matter, left the house with his son, telling his wife they were going out for a while to fit tyres. Instead of heading straight to the tyre fitment centre, he detoured to his concubine's house with his son to spend some time with her. Upon arrival, the poor boy sat quietly on the couch. Overwhelmed by a swirl of emotions as he watched his father cuddle and declare undying love to another woman who was not his mother. On the way back home, the father attempted to silence the boy's confusion and discomfort by buying him a high-tech gadget. He topped it off with cash, manipulating the boy to keep the visit a secret and lie to his mother if she asks any questions.

From this single incident, the child internalizes three powerful lessons:

- ◎ **Duplicity as normal:** He witnesses his father's two-timing behaviour first-hand.
- ◎ **Lying as currency:** He's taught that dishonesty earns rewards.
- ◎ **Complicity as loyalty:** He becomes an acquaintance/alibi, assisting his father in concealing betrayal.

And then we ask: What kind of man will this child become?

Years later, many fathers are dumbfounded when their sons face broken marriages or contract HIV/AIDS. They are quick to label them reckless, irresponsible, and even useless. They have the gall to lash out, forgetting the seeds they themselves planted.

They had soon forgotten that these children had, at some stages in life, witnessed them lying, cheating, and disrespecting their mothers; the very women who nurtured their homes. The deeds of their fathers were construed in a particular manner that seemed normal and acceptable, even. Growing up, these children entered into marriages already doomed to fail from the onset. Many would agree that most of the challenges they experience in their relationships today often emanated from unresolved issues within their families. Those challenges left many wounded inside because they were never dealt with accordingly, and so they never truly healed.

How, then, can we expect these children to grow into adults who respect, love, and remain faithful in their marriages? What are we raising? Cheats, liars, irresponsible and emotionally detached beings? If we truly consider ourselves the responsible parents we proclaim to be, we must lead by example. We must raise children who not only speak the truth but who also live with integrity. That is how we begin to heal our homes; and ultimately, our world. We owe it to our children to be the best parents of unwavering integrity. Parents are the cornerstone of a child's development, profoundly influential to the significant part of their foundational phase.

Let us remember: the pressure we place on our children whether through silence or expectation; shapes the architecture of their emotional world. If we want to raise children who thrive in love, truth, and resilience, we must first confront the patterns we inherited and the ones we perpetuate.

This book is not a condemnation, but a mirror. It invites us to reflect, to heal, and to lead with integrity. The journey begins with us; parents, caregivers, teachers, and mentors; choosing to be intentional about the legacy we leave behind.

So let us raise children who are not burdened by our unresolved wounds, but empowered by our courage to grow. Let us be the generation that breaks cycles, nurtures emotional honesty, and builds homes where truth and tenderness coexist. When we lead with integrity, we don't just raise better children, we raise a better future. A child raised with love and truth will walk through fire and still carry light. My Mom always says: "The truth is hard, but it's the only thing that doesn't break."

The Effect of Bad Upbringing

Grey Area

Foundational Deficit: Dysfunction Upbringing

Early developmental vulnerabilities rooted in poor caregiving and environmental instability

- o Inadequate parental skills
- o Poor decision-making
- o Deficient emotional regulation modeling
- o Impaired autonomy development
- o Exposure to inconsistency or harm

Dark Hole

Adversity Spiral: Chronic Environmental Stressors

Accumulation of unresolved familial and social stressors that compound developmental risk

- o Family feuds and fragmentation
- o Abuse and negligence of children's rights
- o Poverty
- o Lack of support system
- o Absence of protective relationships (e.g., safe adult figures)

Danger Zone

Psychological Fracture: The Breaking Point

- o Loss of self-control and self-identity
- o Social isolation and internalised shame
- o Emotional outburst, withdrawal, aggression
- o Suicidal ideation

Toxic Pleasure

Maladaptive Coping: Toxic Pleasure Seeking

Harmful behaviours adopted as a means of emotional escape or identity compensation

- o Substance use and intoxication
- o Rebellious, volatility, anger dysregulation
- o Anti-social conduct, envy, attention-seeking
- o Distorted intimacy, sexual offences
- o Committing criminal activities

Manifestation

Social & Personal Fallout

Long-term consequences of unresolved trauma and maladaptive coping

- o Chronic failure and disappointment
- o Onset of trauma-related disorders (PTSD, anxiety, stress, depression)
- o Addiction and compulsive traits
- o HIV/AIDS, teenage pregnancy, abortion
- o Narcissistic tendencies
- o Low self-worth and identity confusion
- o Abusive behaviour, physical violence
- o Imprisonment
- o Psychiatric disorders
- o Suicide

Rehabilitation

Rehabilitation & Reintegration: A Fragile Recovery Path

Attempts at healing often hindered by societal stigma and systemic neglect

Win-lose situation

- O Survivors face isolation, societal stigma ,marginalization, and limited support

Relapse

- O High relapse rates due to lack of trauma-informed rehabilitation
- O Society remains insensitive, condemning, persecuting, and rejecting
- O Minimal societal investment in restorative systems
- O Lack or very little rehabilitation support system

Grey Area

The Fragile Foundation

Early developmental vulnerabilities often begin in the shadows of poor caregiving and unstable environments. Inadequate parental skills, inconsistent decision-making, and the absence of healthy emotional modeling leave children without a secure base. Autonomy struggles emerge, and exposure to harm or instability plants seeds of insecurity. This fragile foundation becomes the "grey area"; a place where resilience is possible, but risk is already woven into the child's story.

Dark Hole

The Spiral of Adversity

When unresolved stressors accumulate, the child is drawn deeper into the "dark hole." Family feuds, fragmentation, and neglect of children's rights compound the damage. Poverty and the absence of protective relationships strip away safety nets. Without support, the child faces chronic instability, where every unresolved conflict adds weight to the spiral of adversity.

Danger Zone

The Breaking Point

Here lies the psychological fracture; the breaking point where identity and self-control begin to collapse. Social isolation, internalised shame, and emotional outbursts mark this stage. Withdrawal, aggression, and even suicidal ideation emerge as the child struggles to reconcile pain with survival. The danger zone is where vulnerability becomes visible, yet often misunderstood.

Toxic Pleasure

Maladaptive Coping

In search of escape, toxic pleasures take root. Substance use, intoxication, rebellious conduct, and distorted intimacy become coping mechanisms. Anger dysregulation, envy, and attention-seeking behaviours mask deeper wounds. Crime, volatility, and anti-social conduct reflect attempts to reclaim identity through destructive means. What feels like relief is, in truth, a toxic cycle of harm.

Manifestation

The Fallout of Trauma

The long-term consequences of unresolved trauma manifest in personal and social fallout. Addiction, compulsive traits, and trauma-related disorders such as PTSD, anxiety, and depression emerge. Teenage pregnancy, HIV/AIDS, and abusive relationships reflect the ripple effects of maladaptive coping. Low self-worth, narcissistic tendencies, and identity confusion deepen the struggle. For some, imprisonment, psychiatric disorders, or suicide mark the tragic end of this trajectory.

Rehabilitation

A Fragile Recovery Path

Healing is possible, but fragile. Rehabilitation and reintegration are hindered by societal stigma, systemic neglect, and minimal investment in restorative systems. Survivors often face isolation, condemnation, and rejection. High relapse rates reflect the lack of trauma-informed support. Recovery becomes a win-lose situation, where progress is easily undone by societal insensitivity.

Yet, even in fragility, the pursuit of healing remains a testament to resilience.

Chapter 2

The Dark Hole

Megan's home became a theatre of turmoil, where awful things ensued. She bore witness to injustices and dreadful episodes that had unfolded among her family members. No apologies were ever tendered. Over time, Megan came to accept and perceive the chaos as normal and a way of living. Inevitably, the dysfunction deepened day by day. What she once called love began to twist and transform into something unrecognizable and very horrendous. Peace was a foreign concept in her household. Arguments erupted with alarming regularity, becoming the rhythm of her days. Slowly, these toxic patterns chipped away at her spirit, fraying her nerves.

Megan had no one to confide in. She carried the weight alone. The unrest at home seeped into her studies, and that resulted in a decline in grades at school. Then came the breaking point; the day her whole world came down crumpling and crushed on her; the day she lost her identity altogether. She has discovered the brutal truth in a most gruesome way that no child could ever possibly be prepared for.

On that fateful night, everything unravelled. Her father stumbled in at midnight, drunk and disoriented. In his stupor, he woke her mother from peaceful sleep, and the house erupted into chaos. Their voices clashed in a violent quarrel, echoing through the walls like thunder.

During their screaming match, her dad uttered some words that penetrated very deep into her innocent heart, words sharper than any two-edged sword, piercing until they divided her soul from spirit, and marrow from bones. Her world tilted. Her mind blurred. She stood frozen, unable to breathe. She could feel herself temporarily losing her mind, becoming disoriented and overwhelmed like that.

She stood there motionless after having heard that the man she had loved and believed all her entire life to be her dad was not her biological parent. Can you even begin to imagine the *hurt, the avalanche of disbelief? The how come? Why me? It can't be. These questions raced through her mind.* She cried out, begging her father not to say it one more time, but he did. Each repetition deepened the pain. It was just too painful to hear him saying she is not his daughter. And with each repetition, the pain deepened. Right there and then, she wanted to disappear. She sobbed bitterly, pleading with God to take her life. The rejection was unbearable. It tore a hole in her heart. Nothing could comfort her. She cried uncontrollably, her voice trembling and she collapsed into prayer until all she could utter was: *"God, where are you? Where are you? It hurts so badly. I can't take it anymore; it's beyond my strength. Please, show* up! She cried to God. Where are you? Make it go away, please! It hurts so much; I could die." but the heavens remained silent.

Her father left them. And with him, the last thread of stability unravelled. From that night on, everything changed, negatively affecting her security and welfare. All the curtains of her childhood shut tight before her. Darkness flooded her mind. She became withdrawn and angry. Trust was shattered. The condition in her home intensified from worse to worst, reverberating with pain. She grew bitter toward life.

Each day, Megan woke to a house that felt unfamiliar; quiet, but not peaceful; leaving her emotionally stranded. Her inner monologue stuffed heavy with questions: Who am I now? What does family mean?

Megan often found herself writing letters to her father; not to send, but to reclaim her voice. It became her healing mechanism, and for a while, it worked. Later she began journaling, pouring out her thoughts; not to be read, but to be released.

Here's a tender and emotionally honest version of Megan's first journal entry, written as if she's just beginning to process the trauma; unsure of what healing looks like, but brave enough to begin:

Journal Entry — Day 1

I don't know what I'm doing. I just know I need to write. Maybe if I put the pain on paper, it won't feel so heavy inside me.

Last night broke something in me. I heard things I'll carry with me always. I saw the man I called "Dad" become a stranger. And I became someone I don't recognize.

I keep asking myself: Was it all a lie? The bedtime stories. The birthday hugs. The way he used to call me "my girl." Did any of it mean anything to him? Because it meant everything to me.

I feel like I'm floating outside my body, watching a girl cry so hard she can't breathe. That girl is me. And I don't know how to comfort her.

I begged God to show up. I screamed into the silence. But the silence stayed.

I'm scared. I'm angry. I'm broken. But I'm writing. And maybe that means I haven't given up completely.

If anyone ever reads this, I hope they understand: This isn't just about rejection. It's about identity. It's about losing the one thing I thought was safe.

I don't know what tomorrow holds. But tonight, I'm here. And that has to count for something.

— Megan

After her parents' volatile break-up, her mother did not waste any time before she entered a relationship with Quinton, her new boyfriend, who soon came to cohabit with her into their home just five days after being introduced to Megan. "He's a nice guy," her mother had said, brushing her hair back with a smile Megan hadn't seen in months. Megan wanted to believe her. She really did.

Gradual Unveiling! At first, it was the way Quinton looked at Megan; too long, too often. Then came the touches. It didn't take long before he began to molest Megan sexually. This abuse occurred on numerous occasions while her mother was out gallivanting, or fast asleep due to excessive abuse of alcohol.

Quinton threatened Megan with horrifying consequences if she ever breathed a word to a living soul: *"Say one word, and I'll kill both you and your drunkard mother, and burn the house to the ground."* As if that weren't enough, he manipulated the situation further by accusing Megan of stealing his money. Her mother, blinded by rage and unwilling to hear Megan's side of the story, lashed out violently, hitting and kicking her own daughter as if she were a criminal. And today, we wonder why children in schools attack and kill their peers and teachers, not to mention such an increasingly high rate of violence against women and children. In most instances, these behaviours are mirrored and children emulate such acts from the very adults meant to protect them.

Megan's attempt to expose Quinton's lies to her mother was in vain. Who cared to listen to her? Instead, she was accused of aiming to seduce and snatch her mother's boyfriend from her.

She stopped trying to explain. Words were useless here. Her voice had become a weapon turned against her. So she swallowed it. All these acts of insanity and abuse disoriented the poor girl. She was a wreck emotionally and mentally. She was not okay; she couldn't be okay! At her tender age of 23 years old, her life had already been composed of so many adversities. She had endured calamities and suffered more trauma than most could bear in a lifetime.

As time went on, Megan's body gave in; or rather, betrayed her. It began to reflect the pain she carried. She fell sick. Constant nausea and swollen breasts revealed that something deeper was unravelling within her. She didn't need a doctor to tell her something was wrong. Her body was screaming what her voice could no longer say.

Her mother couldn't ignore the signs. Something was amiss. Suspicion gnawed at her, and by the next morning, she insisted on accompanying Megan to the nearest clinic. A series of tests were conducted, each one inconclusive. Finally, the nurse suggested a pregnancy test. She administered it quietly and returned with the results. Her mother's suspicions were confirmed. Megan was pregnant. Her mother didn't say a word. She simply looked at Megan, nodded once, and turned away.

Megan stood frozen, unable to speak. Shock gripped her, and guilt settled in like a heavy fog. She felt as if she had betrayed her mother. She wanted to apologize, to explain, but she could not get herself to utter a single word. Her mother grabbed her hand; firmly but without anger, and led her out of the clinic. They walked in silence.

All Megan could think was that her mother would surely slaughter her alive once when they reach home. The clinic was just two kilometers away, but that day, the walk felt endless, like a slow march toward judgment. A long walk to freedom, but not the kind Mandela spoke of.

Eventually, they reached home. Quinton was on the couch, watching television. Megan didn't say a word. She went straight to her bedroom and closed the door behind her. She sat on the edge of her bed, stared at the floor. The silence in the house was deafening. She could hear the soft hum of the television in the lounge, but it felt miles away. Her mother's silence echoed louder than any words could. She replayed the clinic visit in her mind; the nurse's glance, the sterile smell, the nod that changed everything.

She felt like a stranger in her own skin. Her body had betrayed her, or maybe she had betrayed herself. She wasn't ready to be a mother. She wasn't ready to face her own. A battlefield raged in her mind; the pregnancy, the shame that came with it, and the sting of disgrace clashed in relentless waves. She was not ready to deal with all of that, not after everything life had already demanded of her. She reached for her journal, the one she hadn't touched in weeks. Her hand trembled as she wrote: *"Today, I became someone else. Not a child. Not yet a mother. Just a girl caught between two truths; the one I lived, and the one I must now face."*

Few moments later, as she sat alone in her bedroom, she heard her mother swearing and screaming at the top of her lungs from the living room. Then suddenly, her name was called. Then, a gentle knock followed. She considered bolting for the hills, but her body was too weak, too drained to move.

Eventually, she said to herself, "Come what may, I am going to walk into the lion's den with my eyes wide open. Let them finish me off for all I care. There is no point in living like this anymore."

Without a word, Megan marched into the living room, her steps bold and defiant. Before she could even sit down, her mother tossed a wad of cash at her and said coldly, "Here. Take this money. Go to Aunt Melinda and fix yourself; fix the mess you've created for us. Make this nonsense evaporate today. And don't you dare breathe a word of this to a living soul."

Megan was stricken by her mom's conniving manner and cruelty toward her. Aunt Melinda? The woman was a she-devil for heaven's sake. She terminate pregnancies for the sake of it and bury the remains in her own backyard. "How on earth can my mother be so inconsiderate?" Megan thought. "In character and conduct, my mother has to be one of the most despicable women alive," She wasn't the best mom in the world, but even for her, this was low and uncalled for. Not that Megan was thrilled about being pregnant or anything. However, when she found out, she had hoped it would finally expose the truth; push her mother to see the monster living under their roof, and drive him out for good.

Unbelievably so, her mother was not even bothered to ask who had impregnated her. Megan knew, with chilling certainty that her mother had always known. Worse still, it's sickening that she had cherry-picked her boyfriend; the man who had been molesting her daughter, over Megan herself. And now, she was defending him at all costs. Megan failed to comprehend it. How could her mother prefer to love and babysit such an older man while sacrificing her own child's safety and dignity? It was a sad reality; one that plays out far too often, especially in blended families.

Is the girl child ever truly safe in these arrangements? Mommy, do you believe your daughter when she tells you your boyfriend or husband is sexually abusing her? Or do you accuse her of lying and refuse to confront the predator in your home?

Are you asking your child to stay silent and simply adapt; merging into your romantic life to keep your partner satisfied and preserve the lavish lifestyle he provides? God forbid.

Too many women lose themselves in the chase for love, neglecting, even resenting their children who need them most. They prioritise their boyfriends, constantly seeking approval, trying to prove their devotion, and choosing them over their children. This kind of desperation is heartbreaking, and must be addressed with serious concern. Could it be that such a woman harbors so much bitterness toward her ex-husband that she now projects that hatred onto the children she shares with him, rejecting everything else that resembles him?

Chapter 3

The Breaking Point

Megan was at her breaking point. She had begun to perceive herself as the problem; the troublemaker in their home. Everything she touched seemed to get ruined. *"Little wonder my dad left us,"* she thought to herself. And then, like a sudden gust of wind tearing through a quiet room, it hit her: "the unresolved mystery behind her sister's death, who had committed suicide four years ago. To this day, no one has ever bothered to sit Megan down to counsel her, or at the very least, attempt to enlighten why her sister had made such a devastating choice.

Though Megan was still very young, she recalled with painful clarity the constant battles between her sister and their mother. However, their father, in contrast, had always taken her sister's side. Today, they are both gone. It's quite disturbing, she sighed.

Dark thoughts began to cloud Megan's mind. She felt herself slipping into a place where life no longer held meaning. Emotionally drained and hollow inside, she was breaking; and no one seemed to notice. No one seemed to care.

Not a single person ever asked her, "How are you feeling today? Are you okay?" nothing of the sort. It was as if all the terrible things that were projected at her throughout her life and had withstood; were invisible, irrelevant. She was expected to gather her act together and carry on as though nothing had happened. Like a good girl, she obeyed her mother's instructions diligently so. The backstreet abortion procedure was carried out as planned, and the rest was buried in silence.

Megan has seen it all at her very young age. Real-life was constantly dragging her down. She was undeniably discouraged, lacking the motivation or hope to become a better version of herself or change her circumstances. Her household conditions chipped away at her confidence and sense of self-worth. She had no one to inspire her, no one to listen, and certainly no one to offer guidance or support. In her community, help was a foreign concept. Instead, people gossiped about her family's dysfunction, using it as a mirror to reflect their own supposed superiority.

She felt insignificant, lost, and all alone as if it was just her against the world. Curled up in her bedroom, she cried through the pain of a relentless migraine. That, on it's own, etched a mind-set of self-doubts, self-limiting beliefs deep into her psyche, making her undermine herself. Negativity consumed her mind.

She began to hear voices whispering cruel affirmations: *"Megan, why even bother? You'll fail. You are a failure; just like the rest of them in your family. Look around. They're all drunkards, illiterates. There's prostitution, failed marriages, unbelievers. Most of your cousins are a bunch of thugs."*

By the look of things, she sighed inwardly. "It is what it is." That old phrase had become her silent anthem. She believed she was cut from the same cloth. I'm no different from them. Therefore, marriage, education, influence were not my portion. Not in this life. "In the absence of light, darkness prevails," they say. And so, she surrendered to the shadows. The poor kid ended up believing the voice of the enemy. Fear and confusion wrapped around her like a fog, leaving her unable to be an active part of her own life. At this point in her life, she became a spectator to her own story. She was convinced that she attracted negative energy like a magnet and that troubles loved her.

One quiet afternoon, Megan sat at home, flipping through television channels with little interest. Her mind was heavy, her heart even more so. Then, something caught her eye; a pastor counselling a mother and her daughter. Something about the scene tugged at her. She leaned in.

The pastor wasn't preaching fire and brimstone. He was listening to them. Gently. Compassionately. He spoke with warmth, offering comfort through the word of God. No judgment. Just love. Megan couldn't look away. She felt something stir inside her; a flicker of hope, maybe. A whisper. *"Could this be the answer?"* she wondered. *"Maybe this is what I need. After everything I've been through... God, is this you? Is this a sign?"*

Normally, Christian channels didn't hold her attention. But this moment felt different. She felt convicted; deeply, quietly. And with a heart full of trembling hope, she made a decision: next Sunday, she would go to church.

It has been a while since Megan stepped into the house of God. The last time she attended church, her sister was still alive; a memory that lingered like a quiet echo in her heart. But this Sunday felt different. Her mind was made up. Without saying a word to anyone, she dressed with quiet determination and left the house. She walked into a nearby church, unsure of what to expect. At the door, an usher greeted her warmly, and the congregation welcomed her with kindness that felt both unfamiliar and deeply comforting.

When the pastor began to preach, his message struck a chord. It was timely, relevant, and pierced through the fog that had clouded her spirit. Megan felt something shift inside her; an almost-peace, a stirring of hope. She knew, without a doubt, she had made the right decision. A quiet pride settled in her chest. At the end of the sermon, the pastor extended an altar call to those ready to receive Jesus Christ as their Lord and Saviour. Megan rose without hesitation. It was a moment of bold surrender; talk about shaming the devil.

Her name was submitted as one of the new converts in need of prayer and counselling. When her turn came, she was invited into the pastor's office. He greeted her with a deeply intimate kind of hug; personal, one that left her feeling seen, comforted, and cared for in a way she hadn't felt in years.

During the session, Megan shared her heart, and the pastor prayed over her with sincerity and compassion. Afterwards, he instructed the ushers to ensure that Megan got home safely; a gesture that wrapped the day in grace.

Later that evening, Megan received a text message from the pastor: "*Good evening, gorgeous! Please find Bible verses that you should meditate on tonight.*" His text messages became her daily dose of comfort. He was consistent, religiously sending her text messages that soon escalated to video calls. She enjoyed the attention. One day, the pastor asked Megan to send him photos so he could pray for her more intentionally. He claimed that God had spoken to him, revealing that she possessed a special gift and needed deeper spiritual covering. Megan grew to be very close to the pastor, often located in his office mainly during the week for her "special prayers." In one of their mid-week meetings, the pastor assured Megan that he would offer her a prominent position in the church, as she was obedient.

Within a week, Megan was promoted to chief usher. The announcement stirred discontent among long-serving members who felt overlooked and unfairly bypassed. Many believed they were more deserving of the role. Despite the murmurs, Megan became the golden girl. With all the privileges and attention she received, she felt safe and content around the pastor. He began to entice Megan with small gifts and would occasionally take her out for dinner, often late after their home visit prayers.

One evening after the home visit prayers, the pastor asked Megan to accompany him back to the church office, claiming he had left his wallet in there. Upon arrival at the church, he insisted that Megan come inside with him. It was dark outside, and he said it was unsafe for her to remain alone in the car. They went in together, and indeed, he took his wallet on his office desk. However, on their way out, something shifted. He gently pulled Megan by the waist, looked deeply into her eyes and said, *"Thank you for coming here with me."* He hugged her tightly, stroked her hair, and let his fingers linger on her face. His hands traced down her neckline, resting briefly on her chest as he whispered how beautiful she was. He told her she deserved to be treated like a queen and that no one in the community could fulfill that role. "I don't mean to pressure you," he added softly, *"but if you allow me, I promise to give you a better life."* Before Megan could respond, he kissed her; passionately and unexpectedly. Then, without another word, he released her and drove her home.

Megan was left in a haze of emotion. She couldn't quite tell how she felt about all of this. She didn't know whether she was incredibly nervous or provoked in that particular manner. She didn't speak of the incident to anyone, nor did she blame him for how things had turned out. As part of their ritual, the pastor continued sending Megan text messages. However, this time his request crossed a line: he asked for photos of her in her bra. Megan was stunned. She chose not to respond to this message.

The next day, they met in the church office behind closed doors. Without warning, he began to touch and kiss her. Megan tried to push him away, but with not much effort awarded. Her denial came as a whisper and her resistance was weak. He had his way with her, and then relieved himself. He told her not to be scared nor mad at him; claiming this was a spiritual confirmation and his way of ordaining her as his future wife. She was the chosen one, he said, and he was simply marking his territory spiritually. He repeated his tired line: *"I am not trying to put any pressure on you or do anything inappropriate. I am not rushing you, and there is no need to divulge the good news to anyone. Let's keep it between us, for now, at least."* From then on, the so-called "ordaining sessions" at the church office occurred almost daily. The church office was no longer a place of prayer. It had never been about prayer to begin with. Megan was expected to provide what he called his "daily antidote," at specified times.

It didn't take long before her world turned upside down. The unthinkable happened! Megan woke up to the devastating news that Pammy, her church mate, had committed suicide. Whispers swirled around the congregation, casting suspicion on the pastor and the circumstances surrounding Pammy's death. Ultimately, to Megan's surprise, what she heard through the grapevine unearthed a bizarre and painful truth: she wasn't the pastor's only concubine. He was only taking her for a ride, just as he had deceived other girls. What she had with him was nothing but a fantasy.

The news drove her over the edge. She stopped attending church. The revelation shattered her. The man she had trusted most had betrayed her, leaving her hurt, ashamed, and deeply disappointed. Pammy's death ripped out her heart. She was in distress. I couldn't protect Pammy," she sobbed. "And now she's gone. I failed her. She didn't deserve this, Megan was inconsolable."

To think she had so much faith in her sister in faith and the pastor; and this happened. Worse still, he ceased communicating with her. He became inaccessible, revealing a side of himself she had never imagined existed. She felt scorned, blindsided by these kind of lies and deceits she hadn't known were possible. In anguish, she cried out bitterly, shouting: *"Then what, God? What is next? Why don't you take me already? Why am I suffering so much in this world? I thought this was your will. I hate this life; I hate church, and I hate all these people. They are cruel and heartless. What have I done to deserve this?"* She collapsed to the floor, sobbing.

Chapter 4

Are we living in the end times?

Megan decided it was time for a change. She sought out a new church, choosing to move forward and embrace a fresh spiritual path. Her decision wasn't just about physical relocation, it was rooted in a deep love for God and unwavering faith in Him. She came to understand that what had transpired between her and the pastor was a personal failing, it had nothing to do with the church itself or with God.

It was during a prayer line that a guest prophet named Miles was ministering, laying hands on members of the congregation, when he encountered Rachel, a striking young woman who had been invited to the church by her friend Megan. Rachel stood patiently in a long queue, waiting for her turn to receive prayer for a breakthrough in marriage. After a while, it was Rachel's turn and she stepped forward with quiet anticipation. Prophet Miles prayed over her, then leaned in and whispered, "You need an intense deliverance." He added, "But right now, here, it's not possible. Meet me at my hotel room at 18:00pm for a complete deliverance session, if you're able. Please be punctual, he requested sincerely. She felt a surge of excitement and counted herself blessed to be chosen by a major prophet to come meet with him for a one-on-one session. Rachel was proactive. She arranged with one of the church's female leaders for her to hang around her place, which is conveniently located directly in the immediate vicinity of the hotel.

As the appointed hour approached and dusk began to settle, Rachel prepared to leave. Shaun, the church leader's son, offered to accompany her. It was getting dark, and his presence brought comfort. Shaun was an usher, kind, obedient, and deeply devoted to God. On weekends, he often stayed at the mission house to assist with housekeeping and prayers.

Together, Rachel and Shaun made their way to the hotel and arrived right on time. Prophet Miles was waiting for them in the reception area. He greeted them warmly and led them to his room. Without delay, he reached for his Bible, read from the Word, and began ministering. Filled with the Spirit, he prophesied over Rachel followed by a concentrated deliverance prayer. Shaun's presence turned out to be a quiet blessing in disguise; he was so pleased with himself for being available to exhibit and serve the prophet with the grace and skill of a seasoned usher. Prophet Miles later thanked him and affirmed that his service in church was indeed a calling.

After closing the session with a prayer, the prophet invited them both to join him for dinner downstairs. Rachel was quick to answer. I thought you'd never ask." Oh yes, we would love to join you for dinner, right Shaun? He nodded in agreement. Okay then, it's settled. Shall we? said the prophet as he led the way. They went downstairs and enjoyed a warm meal together, filled with meaningful conversation. The prophet treated himself to a bottle of wine and he was quick to justify his questionable act with the "Jesus turned water into wine" verse, hallelujah! Rachel also indulged herself in a glass of wine, feeling relaxed and grateful for the evening's blessings.

Time flies fast when you're having fun. They spent a couple of delightful hours listening to the prophet sharing stories from his ministry; moments of triumph, trials, and divine encounters. But as the evening wore on, Rachel glanced at the time and gently suggested they call it a night. Upon saying that, prophet Miles turned to her and politely asked, "May I speak to Shaun in camera? I have a word for him." Rachel nodded, and the two excused themselves from the dining table, heading back to the prophet's hotel room while she remained downstairs in the restaurant.

As Rachel sat alone, she assumed the prophet was prophesying over Shaun. Suddenly, a wild thoughts marathon began racing through her mind. Why would he call aside a 14-year-old minor and deliver a prophecy in the absence of an adult? She wondered. Shouldn't I be there to hear it too, just in case Shaun forgets? I could facilitate in conveying the message to his parents so they'd know what to pray for. But then again, she caught herself. Maybe I'm overthinking this. It's just the prophet and Shaun; boys only, after all. And whatever was said to him might be personal and confidential. I'm not his sister, and I'm certainly not his mother. She sighed, trying to quiet the swirl of questions in her head. Still, something about the situation tugged at her; an unease she couldn't quite name.

Few minutes later, they came back, Rachel was stunned. Shaun was sobbing bitterly, his tears deep and raw, as though he has just lost someone very dear to him. Confused and concerned, Rachel's eyes caught another detail: a stash of cash protruding from the back pocket of his jeans. Clearly, it was from the prophet; he must have blessed him, Megan thought to herself. Still, she was reluctant to ask why Shaun was crying. Something told her not to interfere. It's in God's hands, she reasoned, trying to quiet her unease. Prophet Miles discerned that this situation right here was awkward and Rachel clearly needed an account of some sort. Therefore, he put on a show. He stepped in, hugged Shaun, gently patting his back while locking eyes with Rachel. It was as if he was reassuring Shaun for reasons best known to themselves. Then, in a tender voice, he said to Shaun fondly, "it is well with you my son. You are under my wing now and forever. Do not fear."

They said their goodbyes and off they went. Unbelievably, for a good five- kilometer walk, Shaun and Rachel never said a word to each other until they reached Shaun's home. When they arrived, he walked straight to his bedroom without saying anything to anyone, leaving everyone stunned. They all turned and looked at Rachel, their eyes full of concern, silently seeking for an explanation of his weird behaviour. Rachel tried to explain. I really don't know what to say to you, she admitted. I am equally puzzled as you are. We were all dining with the prophet downstairs at the hotel. As we were about to leave, he requested to speak to Shaun in private.

They went up together to his hotel room. When they returned, Shaun was crying uncontrollably ever since and all the way back home. He hasn't spoken a word since. It doesn't add up. I can only assume the prophecy he received disturbed him deeply. I'm sure he'll confide in you when he's ready.

Shaun's mother was beside herself with worry. She burst into his bedroom, her face pale and tense. Without a word, she locked eyes with her son, searching for answers. Gently, she asked, "What's wrong? He stood up slowly, wrapped his arms around her, and cried his eyes out. His sobs were uncontrollable. Again, she asked, Why are you crying, my boy? What happened? Through trembling lips and a shattered voice, Shaun finally spoke. "Mama... the prophet... he forced himself on me." His words came out in gasps. He threatened to kill me if I tell anyone. He gave me all this money. He said he is a seer, that he hears from God and that he will know if I ever tell on him. Shaun collapsed into her arms, crying hysterically. "He hurt me, Mama. He raped me", and he wept bitterly.

His mother staggered back, her face contorted in disbelief. "Oh my God... how vile!" she shouted in disbelief, clutching her chest as the horror sank in. She called Rachel into the room, her voice shaking. "Come here. You need to hear what Shaun just told me."

Rachel entered the room cautiously. Shaun's mom repeated his confession, her voice raw and broken. Rachel stood there, stupefied into silence. Her eyes widened, her breath caught in her throat. She looked at Shaun, then at his mother, and whispered, "I... I didn't know." But the words felt hollow. She blamed herself. She couldn't speak. Shaun's mom turned away abruptly and stormed into her own bedroom. She grabbed her phone and dialled the local branch pastor. Her voice thundered through the receiver: "That bastard has sodomized my son! I swear, I am going to kill both of you before the police get to you.

I trusted you; I thought you were a man of God, but you're from the pit of hell. Get him over here, now.

Clearly, the pastor was lost and struggled to make sense of what was said to him. However, one thing was clear, this mother was fuming and needed some answers. Her voice cracking with rage and grief as she probed; "So tell me, pastor. Was this planned? Was this a plot to get this bitch here to come over into my house to lure my son into this? You sacrificed my son; for what? Was it money that you sought after? Was it power? Blood? What? Tell me why you have done this, please tell me, and she sobbed uncontrollably.

Then, in a fit of rage, she grabbed Rachel by her weave and lashed out violently, slamming her against the wall, kicking her as Rachel crumpled to the floor. Just as Shaun's mother reached for a vase, Rachel; bleeding and dazed; managed to escape, stumbling out of the house.

The next morning, the headlines were devastating: **Rachel Shozi Found Dead in Apparent Suicide**. Her final words, left in a note, read: *I ended my life because I couldn't find another way to prove I didn't conspire with that false prophet Miles. I never meant to hurt Shaun. How do I begin to take the pain away from Shaun and his family? I blame myself for everything; I am consumed by guilt and shame. I pray that Shaun finds healing, peace and perhaps someday he will find a place in his heart to forgive me."*

In a world where trust is sacred; especially within spiritual spaces; we must remain vigilant. While many pastors and prophets serve with integrity and compassion, there have been heart-breaking instances where individuals in positions of religious authority have abused that trust; particularly in their interactions with young boys and girls.

Let's be clear: blind faith should never replace responsible parenting. It is every parent's and church leader's duty to ensure that children are safe, respected, and nurtured; not just spiritually, but emotionally and physically. This means paying close attention to how pastors and prophets engage with our children, asking questions, and never hesitating to intervene when something feels off.

Transparency must be the cornerstone of any ministry. If a spiritual leader resists collaboration or scrutiny, it raises a critical question: what is being hidden? After all, those who preach truth should welcome accountability.

Let us stand together; not in fear, but in wisdom. This is a call for vigilance in faith communities. Our children deserve safe spaces to grow in faith, and it is up to us to ensure those spaces remain truly sacred.

Chapter 5

Dilemma Concocting Toxic Pleasure

There was no lifeline left for Megan. The church failed her too. The final blow came with two tragic deaths within the congregation, and that was it. Megan walked away from faith for good. Whatever flicker of hope she had clung to; believing someone, somewhere might rescue her and her family; was extinguished. Her home life spiraled into unbearable chaos, a storm of pain and turbulence. Every door she had once believed in had slammed shut. The writing wasn't just on the wall; it screamed in bold, merciless letters: **Negativity. Despair. No escape**. And so, her life took a dark turn. The trauma didn't just shape her; it twisted her. Unfortunately, all of these changed her life for the worst, and her dilemma conceived toxic pleasures in her life.

Megan began to seek comfort in rebellion, immersing herself in all sorts of outrageous behaviours to numb her pain. Out of sheer antagonism, fueled by rage and defiance, she waged the battle of her life. She began to retaliate physically whenever her mother beat her. It escalated to Megan orchestrating a brutal response, enlisting a gang of notorious boys from the neighborhood to "manhandle" uncle Quinton into submission. The boys assured her sarcastically that they would "panel beat" him accordingly and call him to order. Megan watched the aftermath unfold with chilling resolve and the rest was history.

Megan started dating at a very young age, seeking attention and a sense of belonging from boys. Gradually, she resorted to drinking alcohol; first as a social lubricant, then as a crutch. Her act of desperation for attention made her vulnerable and landed her in the hands of older men. They saw her as nothing more than a fantasy to exploit. They dangled money, and Megan took the bait. Having tasted the money "the power of transactional affection," her mind raced with possibilities about the money she could actually earn if she upped her game. Impulsively so, she began to strategise, calculating how to monetize her body with precision and purpose and figuring out how to implement her plan prudently to get laid for money. Streetwise as she was, Megan possessed the skills and attitudes. She identified and studied her target market and areas to target them with ease.

In addition, Megan researched thoroughly and learned the behavioural patterns of her potential major clients. She discovered a secret and what could possibly be a valuable trading weapon for her business: "What drove her clients to want it, and what made them want to spend more money on it." You got to give it to her, "This girl was such an ultimate niche finder, a savvy operator with a sharp eye for opportunity; if only she could channel her dynamism and enthusiasm into the right perspective.

Megan had to improvise and acted fast to come up with her unique marketing plan and a differentiating factor from the other girls (her competitors). But then again, she identified two hindrances that could negatively affect the execution of her plan and make it unsuccessful: the going-to-school part and living at her parents' home. After some careful and much contemplation, her master plan was mapped out perfectly well for her to go live it up out there and in full operation.

She was very content that nothing could impede her plan to prevail. Thus, she started dating whales (rich older men) who were working and well-established financially, strictly so. She has sworn to herself never to date boys her age. She would assertively say to her friends, "Boys my age are sardines and are cramping my style. Hell no, my hot body! No chance, ain't running a loyalty programme nor an early learning centre here. My services are highly specialised and commercialised."

Her plan was airtight. Then came the big move! Megan moved out of the township to share a flat with her friends in the city. School was the first casualty; it derailed her daytime operations, so she dropped out. Most of her loyal and regular clients were married men, so she had to "*balance them*," as she would call it: daytime rendezvous, since at night they had to be home with their unsuspecting wives, playing happy family. These were her classified clients. They paid her handsomely, for as long as she remained discreet about their affair. Her silence was currency and that earned her some oh-so generous incentives. All of that was good accounting for her.

Megan lived large. She had finer things as compared to other girls her age. She owned a car, stayed in a stylish flat, and wore designer outfits. That was a good life; tantalizingly glamorous indeed. Most people envied her lifestyle and would kill for it. Megan thought she had the whole world under her feet. However, in reality, beneath the glamour, Megan's world was unraveling. Her life was in a dilemma; the toxicity seeped into every corner of her life. Day by day, the glitter faded, revealing a girl caught in a storm of her own making; brilliant, bold, and broken.

Chapter 6

The Fall from Grace

As time went by, Megan found herself swept into a love story she hadn't planned. One of her regular whales; charming, magnetic, and unapologetically wealthy had promised her the moon. He swore he would leave his wife, build a life with her, and give her everything she had ever dreamed of. And he was not bluffing. The man oozed luxury. He smelled like money, moved like power, and treated Megan like royalty. Every need? Met. Every whim? Indulged. He adored spoiling her, and she basked in the comfort he curated around her.

Megan didn't just turn heads; she stopped time. She served fashion goals with every outfit, and together, they were the couple that made every social event feel like a runway. She was a celebrity without a portfolio, a muse without a label. She was at that point in life, where her aura screamed abundance. Good vibes and money chased her down, all the way. It found her as though it had her number on speed dial. When people asked, "so what do you do for a living?" she would flash a knowing smile and say, "I am learning money language, and trust me, it is one other language I insist everyone should master besides their native tongue. Why not, it has completely transformed my life. Talk about living my best chapter and being in a good space."

Megan couldn't believe her luck. No one had ever loved her like this man did. He saw her, cherished her, and treated the right way. She enjoyed the attention and completely forgot about the fine line between a client and a lover; it blurred until it vanished. Her heart melted over him; she lost herself helplessly to him. Who wouldn't? He was the kind of man you don't just meet; you encounter. Her friends, green with envy, kept reminding her: "Girl, this one's for keeps." Her love for him deepened with every sunrise. She believed in him and every word that he uttered. Her whole world revolved around him. In her mind, she was his only woman. It was clear that the inconvenient truth; that he was married became a distant echo she chose not to hear.

Megan had a good thing going on for her. Too good. Ten months down the line, the universe gave her a gift: she fell pregnant. She was ecstatic. "Finally! I can give my man the special gift he has always desired," she whispered to herself. He had told her on several occasions that having a child with her would be one of his greatest joys in this lifetime. Megan couldn't wait for him to arrive at her apartment. She wanted the reveal to be perfect. No phone calls. No texts. Just the two of them, in their sacred space. She then prepared his favourite meal. Megan knew so much about food and wine and how best to pair the two. She slipped into her little black dress; the one he loved, the one that made her feel like magic. Then she waited, heart pounding, ready to share the news that would change everything.

After a while, the doorbell rang. Megan's heart skipped. She knew it was him. She dashed to the fridge, poured two half-glass of red wine. She opened the door with a smile that masked her nerves. The rich aroma of wine drifted into the hallway as she walked seductively toward him, slow and deliberate, her eyes locked on his. That moment set the tone for the entire evening; intimate, expectant, electric.

She took off his jacket and led the way to the living room. He sat on the couch while being served with a chilled glass of red wine with practiced grace. Megan curled into his lap, and they cuddled up nicely. She gazed into his eyes and asked softly: "How was your day? Before he could even answer, she reached for her glass. She couldn't keep the news to herself any longer. She sighed heavily, raised her glass high, and asked hastily, "Can I propose a toast?" He raised his brow, intrigued. "Sure, go for it. What's the occasion?" He was curious. "To the new addition to our family," she said, clinking his glass, took a long swallow, and she said nothing further. He blinked. "What addition, sweetheart?" he asked. "Ooh, wait a minute! Did you buy that Chihuahua? Great! But, sweetheart, don't expect me to clean up after him. Count me out. I beg of you," he pleaded with her. "No, silly! It's not about the dog," she said, giggling, shaking her head "Is it not?" His eyes popped out. Now, the poor man was baffled. Without wasting time, Megan blurted it out. "Honey, I'm pregnant!" She gladly revealed it to her loving and wealthy boyfriend. Unbeknownst to her; that day would mark the birth of her predicament and the termination of their honeymoon.

She expected joy. Maybe shock. But not what came next. She found out the hard way that "whales don't want to have babies. Whales only want orgasms, and that is the only service they pay her for."

His face darkened. The warmth drained from his eyes. "You foolish girl, he snapped. How could you be this stupid and reckless? Woman, I mean, couldn't you keep your baby factory closed? I can't be part of this. I'm not, seriously, I don't need it, I don't want any of it. Are you kidding me? What were you thinking? Are you for real right now? Look here, woman; I don't know you. You sleep around with every next guy in town. Who wants a kid with a prostitute? Wait a minute, I know you! I know your type too well."

He reached for his mobile phone. He transferred cash to her via cell phone banking. Her phone beeped to notify her of the deposit. "There you have it! "You understand this language, right?" Go sort yourself out, idiot!" He grabbed his jacket and pointed at her with disgust. "You disgust me! Don't ever contact me!" He stormed out. Megan stood there, shattered. Tears streamed down her face as she watched him drive away with no intention of ever returning to her. He was her financial muscle for Pete's sake, her lover, her illusion of safety. She wanted to run after him and beg him to stay. However, her legs wouldn't move.

At that time, her mind recollected an incident that had occurred in the past. She recalled the day her mother threw money at her to undergo a backstreet abortion after discovering she was pregnant. She was triggered. "Oh, gracious Lord, she sobbed. It's happening again. "My boyfriend just gave me money to perform an abortion!" It's déjà vu." She clutched her stomach. This is a curse, it felt like it. She was convinced that there was an invisible evil force hanging around her determined to rob her of joy, and murdering her innocent unborn infants. But this time, she refused to surrender. "I won't let the devil win," she whispered. She vowed to herself that, as much as this useless and good for nothing boyfriend had dumped her, and left her stranded like this, she would never abort this pregnancy. She strolled toward the door and slammed it. "He is just a little upset. He will come back. He loves me," she said to herself, over and over.

This is his blood I'm carrying, she whispered, touching her tummy. He won't just leave and forget us. I know he will come back. She console herself in that manner each time she cried herself to sleep. Two weeks passed since she broke the news of her pregnancy to her boyfriend, and still, there was no sign of him. It was clear he meant what he said, but to Megan, the reality of it had not yet sunk in. He ceased completely to check up on her; ignored her calls, and vanished into thin air. The silence screamed louder than any insult. Seeing that she was not getting any reaction out of him, Megan resorted to threatening and blackmailing his wife, and still, it didn't work. Frustrated and lost, she had no idea what to do next. She considered reporting him to the police, but she remembered that as much as she was bitter about the whole thing, this was not coercion. It was consensual. She was an adult.

Consumed by rage, Megan became hell-bent on revenge. It wasn't just a thought; it was her mission. She wanted him to feel every ounce of the pain he had inflicted on her, to make him suffer for what he had done. Her mind raced through dark possibilities until a wicked smile crept across her face. "Why didn't I think of this before?" she muttered. Her mind flashed back to her village; back to her original gangsters. The same loyal crew who once battered her mother's abusive boyfriend, Quinton, to a pulp for disrespecting her. *Those boys would die for me*, she thought. Given this assignment, they could execute a clean job. They were good for it. They could silence him for good. No mess. No comebacks. She said it with pride, almost boastfully.

It has been years since she last spoke to them. "Now, how do I get hold of them?" she wondered. Then reality checked in: she had deserted them the moment she moved to the city, becoming important and a socialite. She couldn't be caught dead with low-life scumbags like those. They once met her at a high profile event, and they tried to mingle with her, but she gave them a casual brush off and treated them like total strangers. She remembered vividly how she had embarrassed them that day. The shock and disbelief in their eyes still haunted her. She was not proud of it though, but on the other hand, she couldn't afford to lose her social status and dignity over them. Sadness consumed her, knowing very well that there was nothing she could say to them to excuse her behaviour.

Now, she was alone. Her tummy began to grow bigger and could no longer be concealed behind designer dresses and dim lighting. In her attempt to avoid the shame, she went back on her word and attempted to perform a backstreet abortion. Her plan failed because it was considered a late-term abortion. Even sister Melinda could not help her this time. The whales started to notice her condition. Realising this was not what they signed up for, one by one, they fled. Megan tried to pin responsibility on some of them, but it was all in vain. They all denied her.

This was supposed to be a simple commercial transaction with no strings attached. Men distanced themselves from her. She was left all by herself to deal with the consequences. With no other means of income, she tried to pivot, lowering her standards and making her advances to guys her age. Much to her surprise, even the "sardines" weren't biting. They mocked her, told her to go back to the whales. She was no longer desirable; just a cautionary tale.

Allow me today to advise a girl child: These men aren't loyal, not at all. Don't let them fool you. They are only courting you from the waist down. However, when it comes up there to your face, your mind, your heart, your future; you are on your own and single." So, be cautious about whom you date and their intentions. Only an intelligent and a matured gentleman will open your mind and heart, not just your legs. In sheer desperation, Megan sold her car, trying to maintain the illusion of her former lavish lifestyle. But the stress took its toll on her and the baby, resulting in a difficult pregnancy. The money obtained from selling her car barely lasted until she gave birth to a beautiful bouncing baby girl. Raising the baby all by herself was challenging. The father wanted nothing to do with neither her nor the baby. She was so frustrated. She saw herself as a failure, an idiot, and an absolutely useless person. She could no longer cope, and fell into a depression mode. She attempted suicide, but she was rushed to the hospital, where her life was saved.

The last stroke was when her friends kicked her out of the flat because she could no longer afford to pay rent. Those same friends she had once partied with, laughed with, leaned on; turned against her. As if it was not enough; they told her they could not stand the loud and irritating baby's cry. She was a burden to them and she was no longer in their league. She was now faced with only one unthinkable option: returning to her home village, right back where she started! "Can you even begin to imagine the humiliation? Our unforgiving and so insensitive society!" It was clear that she was going to be a laughing stock. Already, her community had heard of her fall from grace, and they eagerly awaited the "Fallen Queen's" return. Returning home was even harder. The humiliation was unbearable. She had to endure rejection, isolation, condemnation, and ridicule. It's sad how people rejoice over other people's downfall.

In my experience, I would argue that sometimes, the fall is necessary. To some extent; we need to hit rock bottom to find our foundation. The fall can happen for various reasons: to humble us, strip away egos, illusions, and pride. It teaches us compassion, resilience, and truth. People out there are big-headed, inhuman, and need to be humbled and reduced down to size. Therefore, as we surrender to our higher selves, we align with our primary purpose, the right life path, gaining humility and compassion. Some need the fall to strengthen them *now*, preparing them for the heights they're destined to reach. So, when the fall happens again in the future; through persecution, gossip, condemnation, betrayal; they will know how to rise without needing applause, how to endure without breaking, and understand that it is not meant to kill them. So, to every girl who has been hurt, abandoned, or shamed: your fall is not your end. It is your beginning.

Chapter7

Lack of Discernment: The Effect of Bad Upbringing

The provocative questions are, "What happened to Megan? What happened to that ambitious young girl who once had the vision to become a psychotherapist? What killed her Dream? How did she arrive here? Didn't someone notice the self-destructive patterns? As a society, did we stop caring simply because she was not our flesh and blood? Whose fault was it; hers, her parents'?"

Too often, the problems people cause are not the true causes of their problems. They are often the effects of trauma left unhealed. Every day people go through immense struggles, yet few spare time to ascertain why people behave the way they do. We judge the behaviour as the problem without seeking to comprehend the root cause of that behaviour, which is the real problem.

We fail to pay attention, fail to offer a helping hand, yet we are quick to judge and condemn them. People respond differently to hardships. Some fall into a depression mode, some become rebellious, and others act out in ways that seem despicable. But behind each reaction is a cry for help. Due to lack of discernment when coming to the effect of bad upbringing, we do not reach out; instead, we add mountains onto already burdened shoulders. We criticize, exploit, and abandon them in their weakest moments. We distance ourselves from the troubled souls, isolate them and watch them slowly destroying themselves.

With all that is happening in many churches today, we can no longer call churches safe havens anymore. Most of them have become risky places for young women. News headlines reveal a disturbing truth every day: many churches have become breeding grounds for so-called "highly anointed," self-righteous men of God ordained in their own right, misusing their spiritual authority. They desecrate the body of Christ and misrepresent the Gospel of our Lord and Saviour, Jesus Christ. Many of them are actually getting away with unspeakable acts. Look what happened to Megan. What did she do to deserve that?

It is happening right under our noses, yet many remain blind to it due to a lack of discernment to see past the façade. When they look at women in the church, their thoughts are not of ministry or mentorship, but of exploitation. They are strategic and manipulative. They assign minor tasks to targeted women, knowing too well it will bring them into close contact. They lead everyone to believe they are imparting their spiritual gifts unto these women, but in reality, they are grooming these women for sexual abuse as the first step to enslaving them. They befriend these women to gain their trust. They seduce them and often it starts online; luring or coercing women into sending sexual images or videos of themselves; a step in a cycle of control and degradation.

Often young women who had suffered prior abuse, who come from impoverished backgrounds and broken homes, are most at risk of falling prey to these predators; especially within spaces that should offer refuge, like the church. Frankly, most church leaders are quite aware of these violations in churches. They should be the first to protect these young women. Instead, many choose silence to secure their positions and status over justice and compassion.

On the other hand, there are those women who bring mischief upon themselves; a truth that many choose not to acknowledge. These women would see the warning signs or are warned against danger, yet still pursue it. Some young women believe that because their parents are church leaders or financial muscles of the church, they will be treated different. Others think their beauty exempts them from getting a raw deal from church predators. They assume they can have any man they want, particularly those that come with status, money, or power. A young lady once said to this other unemployed brother in church who tried to ask her out: *"Go read your Bible, you will see that the book of Job comes before Romans. Go find a job before you can even think of romancing any woman. There's no romance without finance."* What a revelation! Yet soon after, she found herself in a mess. How do we help someone like this? Already, she is hurt, self-condemning, mistrustful, and worse; blaming God for it because it happened inside the church.

"There is still so much that needs to be done to regulate churches in South Africa. Each time I hear this said, my heart feels ripped apart. When will these systems that are instituted to regulate churches be implemented? Women are being raped every second. Who will save them?

To every girl and woman reading this book: engrave this truth into your heart and mind: The Bible says we are the body of Christ, meaning the church. Therefore, we are the church ourselves. We have been given the power and authority to regulate what happens in the church of God. Such Grace! Let's stand in solidarity and declare: "*I reclaim my power. I am the governor of my own body. In the church, I open my Bible, not my legs. You open my legs, and I open my mouth.*" Ladies, there are no Bible verses written on your breasts, nor hidden inside your underwear. Protect yourself. Be vigilant! Stop looking for many things in the church. Your pastor is not your friend. If he flirts with you, saying you are beautiful and all that. Ask him, "Are you a beautician as well?" Shy away from being alone with a male pastors; this basically protects both parties, prevents accusations and preserves integrity. We applaud and honour the sincere men of God who serve in Truth and in Spirit, preaching the Good news of Jesus and Salvation. May God richly bless you and enlarge your territory in Jesus' mighty name!

People are haunted by their upbringing, by situations known and unknown to us. Truth be told. No one in their right state of mind wakes up and decides to destroy their life and deliberately inflict pain on others. Yes, people tend to be naive to a certain extent, and fall into situations they would regret sooner than later. But what happened to the spirit of "being your brother's keeper?" Where is the guidance, the warning, the love? We live in an era where people watch you walk right into the lion's den and still keep quiet, or not even warn you at the very least.

Troubled souls often try to reach out, but no one notices. People are far too busy, far too self-absorbed. Worse, there're these odd types of people who spend their precious time monitoring your life closely; not to help, but to witness your downfall. They watch you ruin your life; if not helping the situation. They keep records of your mistakes, waiting for the day you turn to them for help, just so they can say, "*I told you so.*" People can be so unforgiving; you can take that to the bank. They will push you right to the edge, to the point of no return.

As much as Megan has misbehaved, as much as we have witnessed every outrageous thing she has done and as much as she is going through a rough patch; we may say she deserves it. But what if her toxic and outrageous behaviour are a reaction to the trauma she endured growing up? What if her pain is speaking through her rebellion? Wouldn't the world be a better place if we analyse and focus on the causes of the problem rather than focusing only on the problem itself? By doing so, we would understand ourselves better and be able to reach out to others with empathy, not judgment.

Chapter 8

#Latepost – Refuse to Be One!

I dare you; refuse to be a #Latepost for the life in you. Die a hero. Don't miss your destiny. Rise to the occasion, show up, and unleash the best version of yourself. Make it in this life through sweat and pain. No one said it was going to be easy; we all have to keep on grinding. Leave a legacy! Make your mark and engrave it in time.

In social media terms, a #Latepost is when a photo or post is uploaded long after the moment has passed. But in this context, #Latepost implies something far more tragic: it's when your supposed friends and family only start posting about you on social media, social gatherings; sharing memories, tributes, and stories after when the inevitable and painful events have happened to you, like death, job loss, divorce or addiction. Suddenly, everyone has something to say: How they knew you during your heydays, how they were very close to you, how much they loved you and how they wish they could have saved the situation. But where were they when you needed them? The truth is, you meant nothing to them while you were alive and struggling. They couldn't care about your challenges and the bad things that could happen to you. All of a sudden, they want to be perceived before the eyes of the public as good Samaritans. Don't be surprised! Some will speak well about you, and others will tarnish your name publicly because there is a specific benefit that comes with it in terms of monetary value, or simply a chance for them to scoop a spot in the limelight.

Your life, all of a sudden, will become interesting and even worth being documented. You'll be a trending topic. You'll become another statistic or another case study. Your sorry or lifeless face will be disgraced, broadcasted and gracing your enemies' TV sets at the comfort of their home, pub screens, and across social feeds. You will be known; but it will be a bit too late as you will be dead. You are not Jesus; your death will not redeem anyone or have lasting impact. It will be in vain.

Those friends you spent all your time and money trying to impress, those you bent over backwards to please and conforming to their set standards. They will be the very ones telling people how useless you were. Sadly, that is the true nature of the typical society we live in. People are not celebrated while they are still alive for their good deeds. Folks are too quick to say RIP to the dead but tongue-tightened when it comes to saying congratulations to someone who is prospering. Seemingly, it becomes hard for people to accept and embrace other people's success; rather, they sabotage them and await their downfall.

❖ Watch out; it's a trap!

Have you ever felt like the life you are living is not yours? Like someone out there is living your life, hijacked your destiny forcing you to live a pathetic existence full of sorrows you are currently facing? That is exactly how Megan felt. Though we cannot blame it all unto the poor devil; however, he is the culprit in most instances behind the scenes, so we cannot entirely vouch for him.

As we grew up, in our ideal world, we had everything figured out; how we desired our life to turn out: the perfect marriages we wished for, the thriving businesses and careers, and taking over the world by storm! If only it were that simple, everything would be great and grand, you know! But then the inevitable happens. Without warning, your whole life takes a new and detrimental turn. Everything shifts. You find yourself in no control of anything and having no say over anything. All you see are your flaws turning into a raging bull inside of you, terrorising the living daylights out of you. You don't even know how to fix it or where to turn to for help. That's when you realise: we effortlessly dream the most daring and colourful dreams; for free; but life itself has it's own agenda for us.

Watch out; it's a trap! Refuse to believe otherwise. You had a vision of yourself; making it big in life. That's your starting point. Stick to your guns. You can still turn your life around and live the life you have always desired for yourself. Never allow your background or current circumstances to dictate your future. Don't let them discourage you from executing your action plan to realise your dream.

Chapter 9

The Turning Point

During her absence from home, the living conditions there deteriorated drastically. Upon returning home, Megan found her mother more deeply immersed in the dating scene than ever before. She would leave Megan behind to stay with her boyfriends, and only returning home on weekends. Megan was left alone to fend for her baby brother and her own daughter. Juggling the roles of a sister and a mother overwhelmed her, and she could barely cope.

This abandonment was not just irresponsible; it was dangerous. Leaving this poor girl all alone, poverty-stricken, burdened with adult responsibilities like that could only trigger or pose risk of Megan falling prey to older men as a survival mechanism. In this era, troubling survival mechanisms have emerged, where young girls exchange intimacy for money, often with the silent consent of parents who are unemployed, widowed, or desperate. Some even encourage their daughters to engage in covert relationships with their best friends' husbands or relatives' spouses, just to put food on the table. It's shocking; and closer to home than we think. It could be someone in your own family, silently struggling to make ends meet since they were retrenched three years ago. Do you care to know what is happening to them lately? When was the last time you bought bread for them? Paid them a visit without judgment, gossiping or comparisons; like whose children attend private schools? Have you asked how they're really doing?

We need to rise above this kind of ignorance. The way these young girls are forced to live now will shape how they view relationships in the future. Let's raise responsible men and strong, independent women who can live safely and freely among one another.

Many times, Megan wanted to flee from home to resume her old lifestyle. However, she realised that a lot had changed. She was a mother now. She couldn't bear the thought of deserting her daughter with her mom. Yet as a harlot, bringing her child into that world of desperation and exploitation was equally unthinkable. She fought with her thoughts. She was trapped; emotionally, mentally, and spiritually; and it all simply came to what seemed to lead to a cul-de-sac for her.

As time passed, something beautiful began to bloom. Megan bonded deeply with her daughter. She loved her fiercely, more than anything in this world. She loved being a mother and found joy in caring for her child. She was doing amazingly well as a mother; much better than her mother was to her. She desired a better life for her child.

Motherhood transformed her. Her priorities shifted. Every decision she made was for her daughter's future.

Megan was fiercely protective over her daughter. No one was allowed to touch her child, and that was something her mother failed to do for her. The fear of not being able to provide for her child haunted her. At night, her mind raced with worry. It was killing her inside. She was terrified that, as a result of lack and poverty, her daughter might resort to the same destructive path she had once walked.

Her heart was teeming with regrets. She condemned herself. Dropping out of school left her without qualifications. She equated herself to her peers, which deepened her sense of inadequacy and feeling left behind. Everyone around her acted superior, as if she were beneath them. They dismissed her, wrote her off and believed it was over for her. Some parents went to such an extent that Megan's name was used as a point of reference when reprimanding their misbehaving children. Others forbade their children from associating with her entirely. The rejection and the constant judgements were relentless and uncalled for.

After everything that was said and done in an attempt to destroy Megan; after all the humiliation she suffered, the serene prayers whispered and the countless nights she cried herself to sleep; something shifted. One morning, she simply woke up and decided that *she was done.* Done living in bondage, done crying endlessly, done feeling sorry for herself, and done giving her haters the satisfaction of watching her dance to their tune. She then said to herself, *"It's not worth it, all of it. If it doesn't bring me solutions to my current predicament, why torture myself? I'm only jobless, `single parenting with no friends, but as surely as*

God lives, I'm not disabled. I still have my brains, and I can transform and put it to good use."

As she was laying down on her bed, lost in thought and silently praying; she sank into the mattress, the weight of her thoughts pressing heavier than the sheets around her. Then, like a tide retreating from shore, a wave of peace washed over her; quiet, steady, and unexpected. Suddenly, her mind, once crowded with noise, softened into stillness. Hope bloomed and she felt her strength being renewed all over again. She felt the joy of the Lord fill her spirit, and she knew without a doubt that this was divine. She realised that by uttering boldly and declaring her will to rise, she had taken a leap of faith. She knew right there and then that *"it could only be God."* For the first time in her life, she felt true peace. She felt she was on the winning side. God was with her. Mercy had found her!

You see, when you embark on a journey of self-introspection, healing and self-correcting, you need to involve God to hear what He is saying about your situation. He will guide you, renew your strength and help you overcome daily despair. This self-recovery journey is a tricky process. Many start strong, only to fall into despondency and abandon the mission prematurely; landing right back where they started. And when that happens, picking yourself up again feels nearly impossible. The burden grows heavier. That is why you will need support through this journey; whether from your parents, a certified counselor, or your pastor; to walk with you and offer guidance.

We live in a society where many parents have stopped caring about what unfolds in their children's lives; just like Megan's mom. One fallout with them, and it's over.

They disown their children and send them packing out to the vultures. They make no effort to comprehend the pain or the underlying causes behind that led to their children's behaviour. Imagine Megan's reality. Her mother was present, yet Megan suffered under her hands. She was the prime instigator behind Megan's ordeal. To make matters worse, when society added its own layer of humiliation and condemnation, it was just too much for her to bear. The poor girl felt utterly alone; just her against the world. I often find myself asking: What has this world turned into? Do we bring children into this life only to watch them suffer? How can we conceive and bear children out of the act of love, and then perceive and treat them as enemies, wishing them dead?

One rainy afternoon, as Megan stood outside the local clinic waiting for her daughter's check-up, soaked and clutching a threadbare umbrella, an older woman approached her. She was a retired teacher named Mrs. Dlamini, known in the community for her stern demeanor and no-nonsense attitude. Megan braced herself for yet another judgmental glance. Instead, Mrs. Dlamini gently placed her own sturdy umbrella over Megan's head and said, "You're doing well, child. I see you. I see how you carry that little one with love. Don't let anyone tell you you're less than." Megan was stunned. No one had spoken to her like that in years; especially not someone like Mrs. Dlamini.

The woman reached into her handbag and handed Megan a small envelope. *"It's not much,"* she said, *"but I want you to buy something warm for your daughter. And if you ever need help with schoolwork or anything, come by my house. I still have my books."* Tears welled up in Megan's eyes. That simple gesture; a dry umbrella, a few rands, and an offer of support; pierced through the fog of shame and isolation. It reminded her that not everyone had written her off. Some people still believed in second chances.

As she clutched the envelope, Megan felt something stir inside her; a flicker of warmth she hadn't felt in a long time. Maybe life hadn't closed its doors completely. Maybe, just maybe, this was the beginning of a new chapter. The kindness of a stranger had cracked open the possibility that healing was still within reach. She didn't have to stay stuck in the past. She could rise, slowly but surely, and rewrite her story; not just for herself, but for her daughter too

Chapter 10

Deactivate the Code of Failure

Deactivating the code of failure is not a one-time decision; it is a deliberate, soul-deep process. It begins with identifying, incapacitating and decisively dealing with every stronghold within you and in all other aspects of your life that suppress your spirit and stunt your growth. These are the internal forces that daunt you, distract you, and keep you from reclaiming your life. Our code of failure differs from person to person and it is not necessarily a list of past mistakes; those you have long done and they have already burned their lessons into you. The actual code of failure, as defined by the author, Pinky Thompson, means the invisible battle within you, with yourself fighting against your own thoughts, slowly poisoning your morale, chipping away at your confidence, and quietly convincing you that you are not worthy of change. And as a result it unconsciously disables you from being an active agent of your own life. It is those emotions of feeling rejected, fearful, hurt, seeking validation and approval from others, not wanting to try anymore to break new grounds, and the self-condemnation. Eventually that builds, bit-by-bit a web of lies and illusions, inaccurate notions, and misperceptions about yourself. All of these dynamics are the strongholds; the code of failures in your life that you must to deactivate rigorously.

For Megan, the urgency was real. She had to turn her life around; for the sake of her baby, if not yet for herself. But each time she tried to take a step forward to improve her life, her track record spoke against her. The condemnations from others were awful. Her past life overshadowed every effort to do well. She had no personal support system. Her baby was her only anchor; the only light that motivated her to want to do better for both of them.

Megan has been a victim of family feuds, abuse, and molestation. She bottled it all up, but when provoked, rage erupted like a volcano and she would bounce back with great vengeance. She was overprotective of her daughter. She could never stand anyone touching her. She lived in isolation, trusting no one. Everyone was a suspect. Deep down, she knew something was wrong with her, but she had no idea and couldn't quite put her finger on it. It was like chasing shadows in her own soul.

For her to unlock her value and potential, Megan decided and put in a conscious effort to accept that she could not change what happened to her. However, she could do something about it; to shape her future. That meant choosing to rewrite her story by facing her mistakes, and identifying her weaknesses that had in the past triggered or stimulated destructive behaviour that led her astray. Megan came to *realise* that, what held her back was no longer her past. Eventually, she ***identified*** the real problem: It was not the fact that she had committed abortion; it was not the fact that she was sexually molested; it was not because she had been a prostitute, neither was it all those despicable toxic pleasures she had once affianced herself to. The primary cause that pulled Megan backward was *self-condemnation.* She had sentenced herself to a life of emotional imprisonment, allowing shame to build walls around her and set limitations to herself by allowing people define her worth.

To break free, Megan had to confront herself. She had to wrestle the monster within her; the voice that whispered she wasn't enough. She had to break every chain, tear down every lie, disarm every fear, incapacitate every stronghold in her life to liberate herself and reclaim her power. That was when Megan discovered that the toughest battle you'll ever fight in your life is the battle within yourself: between who you are now and who you want to become. Unfortunately, there are battles you will have to fight even when you feel defeated already. They demand mental strength you didn't know you had and always leave you with an ultimatum: *force yourself to push through a challenge and eventually overcome the obstacle, or you succumb to pressure; quit, and be defeated.*

To get to the core of your strongholds, you must probe and ask yourself the hard questions: *"What are the constant battlefields in my life? What unhealthy habits or thought patterns have a stronghold over me?"* Only then can you begin the work of liberation.

❖ How to Deactivate the Code of Failure

❏ The Lie of Unworthiness

Deactivate the feeling of unworthiness. Unworthiness is a lie the world tries to sell you. Society has a tendency to make one believe that they are worthless and can never rise above it's set standards and expectations. People have opinions about everything, and everyone alright! Haters will weaponise your past mistakes, hoping you'll turn against yourself and question your value. But here's the truth: *you are not your past. You are not your failures.* Stop discrediting yourself. Stop condemning yourself. Train your heart to let go of everything you fear to lose. Love yourself and be kind to yourself. Give yourself some grace by forgiving yourself. God has already forgiven; you for every slight misstep, every sin committed knowingly or unknowingly. You have to quit being hard on yourself. Perfection is an illusion. Embrace your imperfections; you can only learn from your mistakes, for all their worth. Make the tough calls you are afraid to make. Have a vision. Know your strength and weaknesses, and start working on them. Have a game plan and just do it, and for some extra motivations, do it simply to spite the enemy because they said you couldn't do it. *I pray for you that: "You shall start and you shall finish well. You will not quit half way and surely, you will not die before your purpose is fulfilled, Amen.*

❏ Feeling Inadequate

Feeling inadequate is one of the worst feelings ever. Inadequacy is a thief; it steals your joy, isolates you from the people who love you, and convinces you that you don't belong. Giving into it can overshadow every good within you.

Rule number 1: Make it a mission to avoid people who pull you down and justify it by their own inadequacy. Don't allow it. Don't sink with them; you will drown in sorrow. Keep the feeling of inadequacy at bay.

Rule number 2: Don't project your feelings of inadequacy onto others.

Rule number 3: Expand your knowledge; it will set you apart from the rest. Try out new things; join a book club, go hiking, or learn a digital skill. Interact more with people who encourage you, keep your head floating, and help you see the broader picture. Write down all your strong qualities and revisit them whenever that feeling of inadequacy consumes your thoughts. Every one of us is unique and gifted in something. Broaden your horizons!

❑ Lack of Accountability

Do not let life pass you by. Stop wasting time blaming other people for your failures, Acknowledge and accept that you have messed up. Account for your mistakes, apologise, fix what you can, learn from them, and prevent them from happening again. That is accountability. Do not let people guilt-trip you; it is very far and expensive. Owning up to your mistakes shouldn't cost you your blood; if it does, walk away, and let peace be with you. At times, it can be emotionally exhausting to prove daily to people that you are sorry, especially when people refuse to give you the benefit of the doubt in return. Mind you; people are not as forgiving. Being in pursuit of their forgiveness can delay and derail your progress. The best remedy is to acknowledge your wrongdoings, own up to them, and prevent them from recurring.

❑ Overthinking – the Worst Enemy of Mankind

You are an inventor; destined for bigger and greater things. Who knows; you may one day invent a cure for HIV/AIDS? But how will you be able to execute such a plan if your mind is not creative, always clouded with negativity and self-condemnation? The enemy uses distractions to consume our thoughts. When the mind is overthinking, clouded, overwhelmed by negativities, it becomes your worst enemy. It poisons the way you think, how you perceive things. It distorts reality and create problems that do not exist at all. Feed your mind with sensible thoughts that can even earn you some extra income. These days, people are paid to think; so think wisely.

Do not be caught dead on the web of those people who spend their time obsessing over others' success. Are they paying you? Focus on yourself. Everything begins in your mind. Be creative and invent the best version of yourself. Rather instead of worrying, channel your energy into becoming that fashion designer, software developer, or whatever dream you hold. If you work on it, it will come to pass.

❑ The Trap of Seeking Validation

Do not dance to the haters' tune. Do not seek their approval. They have their own flaws and blunders. They have failed in life, and they will make you believe you are a failure too. They will make you feel compelled to explain your every move to them for their stamp of approval. Do not succumb to their pressure. Most of them are losers in their own right.

People will not always believe in your vision; and it is within their right, but it is your vision. Make it happen for yourself and let others lose sleep over your success. It is not the haters' duty but yours to love and believe in yourself and your dreams. Seeking validation from others is costly. Stop doubting yourself. Stop seeking approval. Put your energy toward achieving your goals. Believe in your ability to make the right decisions. Go with what looks and feels right for you.

❑ Inheriting Problems

Inheriting other people's problems was exactly what happened to Megan. She overburdened herself with her parents' struggles, believing she came from a family of failures, and due to her background; was therefore a failure by default. In life, we all encounter challenges. However, never allow yourself to inherit the problems of others, especially your parents. Yet, sometimes, we have no choice. Circumstances surrounding our upbringing make us to be acquainted with our family problems, our parents, and impulsively, we inherit those problems. Nonetheless, be the kind of person who says: "*Whatever conquered my parents shall not conquer me!*" Your parents' mistakes are not yours. Set goals for yourself and be the first one to accomplish accolades that no one in your family has attained. You are unique, and you can make a difference. Be the light of your family. In bad situations, disregard the bad and inherit only the good.

A certain pastor once shared a story in his sermon. He spoke of a drunkard uncle who lived immorally but was wealthy and owned a Rolls Royce. Looking at his uncle's life, he asked himself: "What is it that I am learning from my uncle?" This was because immoral things surrounded his uncle, leaving little to be desired? The pastor said he then concluded to inherit the good from his uncle and leave the bad. On that note, he made a declaration, "The anointing of drunkenness I do not inherit, but the anointing of Rolls Royce I receive." Choose wisely what you inherit.

❏ Refuse to Be Oppressed

Refuse to be oppressed at all costs; especially by those who are oppressed themselves. People out there are mentally and economically oppressed, and allowing them to influence you can take its toll on you, causing you to regress. Never lose focus. Be consistent, committed and true to yourself. The mentally oppressed people live in bondage; slavery, anger, hatred, bullying, stagnation, and so forth. Having suffered oppression, they ensure that they inflict the same pain on others as well. They can't get themselves out of their own misery, so they use your mistakes to paint them to you as the worst and unforgivable sin ever, shifting focus away from themselves. They can never be happy for anyone. They enjoy seeing other people suffer. Meet them at the workplace, when such people are in authority; they will show you hades. They will oppress you, disregard your ideas, and make it their mission to stunt your growth within the company.

They always undermine, bully, and compete with others; though in reality, they are in competition with themselves. They are unworthy of wasting your time and energy in fighting them. It's a battle you cannot win; it's deep and psychological. Just forgive them for every wrongdoing.

Already, they are suffering, and miserable inside. You only have to wish them healing.

God will assign you destiny helpers. You will meet and have an encounter with different kinds of people before reaching the land of promise. When you meet the oppressor, he will find you in peace and leave you in pieces. However, your destiny helper will find you in pieces and lead you to peace and your breakthrough.

Beware of poverty-stricken minds. Those are the most dangerous people you have to guard against. They are used to having nothing and doing nothing to achieve something. For them, everything is difficult and unattainable. They fold their arms, look at a task or situation, and conclude in their minds, that it is not their portion. They wouldn't dare lift a finger to try. They complain, hate, oppress, and discourage those striving toward their goals in life. Isolate yourself from such people. They have a problem for every solution and attract poverty. Protect your peace.

Call to Action: Start today. Choose healing. Choose growth. Choose YOU.

Chapter 11

Decoding the Past

Decoding the past is a mental, emotional and academic ability to analyse your life's failures, adversities, and painful experiences to name a few to transform them into creative, meaningful lessons that can bring about a renewed, purposeful existence. It can be a hard and traumatic exercise for others even to try, as it means revisiting the past wounds that were long buried, confronting truths that were easier to ignore. Hence, at the beginning of this book, I emphasized that one needs to decode past failures with accuracy and compassion. That's exactly what Megan did.

She began the process by forging a goal-oriented life out of what had once seemed to be a condemned and futile life. She reminded herself daily: *"I've already suffered humiliation and abuse. I'm hurting because I've lost everything; my virginity, dignity, my sister, and my father. I have nothing left to lose in trying and failing at this point. Nothing can scare me anymore. It can't get worse than it already has."*

It should not be taken for granted the fact that Megan was able to reach this stage. This was no small feat; it was a milestone that demanded every fiber of her being. It was a break-even point where life altering decisions had to be made. The type of decisions that would directly impact her future. Whether good or bad, she would have to live with them. That is why, at this juncture, it is important to understand what contributed to your setbacks and destructive patterns. What role did you play; whether by allowing, encouraging or even self-inflicting the pain or damage you now suffer? You must be true to yourself. Only then you can begin to subdue and overcome the strongholds that oppress your mind and steal your joy. Probing, interrogating and unpacking your situation from that angle, exposes the problem at its core. It brings clarity. It helps you determine what kind of decisions must be made to move forward. And here is where many people begin to regress. They've grown accustomed to living a life that is full-centered by a web of lies, pain and continuously comforted by more lies rather than the truth. They are petrified to live outside of their safe haven, even when they know liberation awaits. That fear impedes progress. It keeps them stuck in cycles of avoidance, denial, and self-sabotage.

People often dread starting something new or setting boundaries against what has been causing them pain. They fear that letting go will expose their vulnerability and reveal that they were gullible. They worry it could invite loneliness and condemnation; and for many, that feels unbearable.

All of these projected fears are entirely understandable. They are deeply human. Therefore, in the midst of it all, be encouraged. Do not despair; do not be afraid to make those important and liberating decisions. Relapsing now won't solve anything. Instead all your burdens will resurgence and mushroom into mountains and storms that threaten to overwhelm you; if not finishing you off. Be one-step ahead. Take it up with God, for the battle is not yours. God himself, the giver of life is saying to you:

Isaiah 41:10 - "So do not fear, for I am with you; do not be dismayed, for I am your God. I will strengthen you and help you. I will uphold you with my righteous right hand."

Isaiah 55:11 - "God is not a man that he should lie. So is my word that goes out from my mouth: It will not return to me empty, but will accomplish what I desire and achieve the purpose for which I sent it."

Matthew 24:35 - "The heaven and the earth will pass away, but My words shall not pass away."

Truly, you have no reason to fear. You are heavenly protected and you are being upheld by a promise that cannot fail.

❖ Decoding the Past in 11 Steps

1. Model your life

Megan came to a pivotal realisation: she needed a plan to shape her life into something meaningful and productive, to be a role model to her daughter and to serve as a source of inspiration to her peers. She was prepared to decode the past and do whatever it would take. She recalled the fierce energy she once had while strategising previously as a prostitute. Back then, she exhumed her drive from within. That same drive still lived within her. But this time, she would redirect it; re-strategising with intention, channeling her initiative into a constructive game plan that not only accommodate her present reality but also pushed her toward her best self.

Finally, after some long and hard introspection, Megan was able to define her goals and mapped out a plan toward her personal growth. Her top priorities were learning new skills, enhancing her quality of life and working toward her dreams. She applied for jobs as a general worker and intended to enroll in part-time courses, should her job application be successful. In that way, she could afford to take her child to a day-care centre. She was enthusiastic about the future.

Things began to align. She realised that God was never silent on her. All these years, she was not asking God; she was only crying and not crying unto God. She was impatient and never allocated herself some time to hear from God. She acted out of her own carnal mind. And that was not, and never was the will of God for her life.

Mental and Emotional Readiness

Megan realised that for her to succeed through this transitioning journey of reinventing herself, it required full acceptance of change. She had to let go of her former life completely. She began brainstorming and writing down every feasible idea; steps she could take to reach her goals. She was brilliant and realistic in accepting that it wouldn't be an easy process. It was never going to happen overnight. Yet she was convinced and confident. She believed in the process and committed to taking it one step at a time. Megan had to prioritise and plan around her time, drafting a to-do list to manage and execute her action plan. Though unfamiliar, she embraced the challenge. She prepared herself mentally, emotionally, and physically. Being fearful was not even an option. She repeatedly meditated, training herself to grow accustomed to uncertainty and discomfort.

3. Mental Health Awareness

As a society, we need to educate ourselves more and always strive to become more conscious of mental health issues. Our youth are the most vulnerable. Many suffer silently with mental health problems such as anxiety, depression, bipolar disorder, or insomnia, and face a heightened risk of suicidal thoughts. Parents, tutors, and employers should foster open conversations about mental health awareness. Assuredly, this drive will help prevent and reduce the alarming statistics around depression among youth, which in most cases, lead to suicides. None of us are immune when it comes to the encounter with life's inevitable hard knocks. That is why we must encourage open talks on mental health awareness, sharing our stories, and support one another. Talking about the adversities you have encountered, and how you overcame them; could save someone else's life.

Megan felt herself slowly losing her sanity, so she sought professional help. Seeking professional help is never in vain. Forget about those narrow-minded people who stigmatise everything. Let me enlighten you: they too, go through rough patches in life; quietly and discreetly, they often seek professional help without thinking twice. The goal is survival, healing, and restoration. In the face of adversity, stay positive. Have faith and tell yourself, *"This situation won't take me to the grave. This, too, shall pass!"* Find yourself and become your better self.

Wellness is not a task; it is a way of living. Feed your body with food that nourishes and strengthens, exercise regularly and get enough sleep. Do not drive yourself into exhaustion; even the strongest vessel must pause to float. Surround yourself with loved ones. And above all, discover the miracle of giving. When you lift another soul, you rise with them. Reach out to the destitute, the disabled, and the elderly widows who lives alone. Give to the needy. Allow yourself, for once, to forget about your own circumstances and help someone. Offer your time, your hands, and your heart. That moment when you become someone's lifeline; knowing that they were dying and in need to be saved by an angel, and you became one to them that day; it's priceless. At times, the answers we seek come when we least expect them. Solution to our problems often tend to unfolds as we help others, because we let go of our own negativity energy. The universe has it's own way of returning goodness; not always through the same people we have rescued, but in ways you least expect.

4. Decoding your thought before sleep

Remember that the last thought you have before sleep can linger in your subconscious mind for up to four hours. Your last waking perception of yourself mostly dominates your slumber. Each night before you drift off to sleep, choose to replace your fears, worries, and disappointment by dwelling on positive thoughts or affirmations. These will be reinforced in the hours of being immersed in your subconscious mind. Create a bedside reminder like a prayer, a mantra, or a declaration of faith. Speak life into your subconscious. Speak healing. Speak victory.

5. Rebuild your reputation

Megan came to terms with the fact that she was not an angel, and she had a track record to show for it. She realised that her past could work against her future plans. However, she never allowed that to hold her back. The first step she took was to deprogram every past behavioural pattern. She began to lead a clean and honest life. She was bent on becoming a new person and rebuilding her battered reputation.

She knew it would be challenging to convince the world that she was now a reformed person. But rebuilding her reputation wasn't about convincing the world; it was about proving to herself that she was trustworthy, transformed, and worthy of respect. She wanted to be the change that this world needs to see. Her attitude was clear: *"If anyone still holding on to my past, by all means, let them play that old broken record all they want. I've moved on. I've decided."*

6. Overcoming your fear

Fear works directly against faith. When you are fearful, you can't think properly. You end up making irrational decisions. Megan chose faith over fear. She understood that living in faith meant stepping boldly into new opportunities, and making life-changing decision to better your life. Fear is the opposite of faith, plain and simple; just as much as there's a difference between good and evil. Remember, fear is the spirit from hell. *2 Timothy 1:7, "For God hath not given us the spirit of fear, but of power, and love and of a sound mind."*

So what do we do when we find ourselves living somewhere between faith and fear, (hopefully more toward the faith end)? Megan vowed that having been given a second chance to turn her life around, she would experiment and venture into new projects lined up in her life without fear. She made up her mind to grab every opportunity that came her way with two hands and make the most of it.

7. Feed your mind

What are you feeding your mind with? Insecurities, negativity, jealousy, pornography? Megan chose to nourish her mind with knowledge. She read books, attended seminars, and opened herself to new ideas. This was an eye-opener for her. It assisted her acquire a wealth of knowledge to build and strengthen her belief system. Knowledge is power, Francis Beacon said. Through reading and attending seminars, Megan became more enlightened than ever before. She was truly blessed indeed by these experiences.

One day, Megan discovered privileged information regarding a free computer course that was offered for six months. She seized the opportunity and enrolled. That helped her grow both personally and professionally. A well-fed mind is confident, motivated, and open to transformation. It develops mental skills with ease, introducing you to new people and new thoughts. Feed yours wisely.

8. Outlook on Life

Your outlook on life is a direct reflection of how much you value yourself. Folks who don't depend on others for their main source of happiness radiate joy and confidence. They crush on themselves every day. People who love themselves are happy with themselves. Can you fall in love with yourself? Can you embrace the person God created you to be? When you love yourself, you learn to forgive yourself. When you forgive yourself, you learn to respect yourself. When you respect yourself, you learn to value and know your self-worth. When you value and know your self-worth, you discover your primary purpose and live a more liberated, fruitful and an empowered life. People will see who you are and treat you the right way. Most importantly, they will honor your values and goals.

9. Seek mentorship and be coachable

You weren't meant to do this life thing alone. On your own, you may stumble, but with guidance you can rise. Find a mentor; someone who has walked the path you're now on and can guide you step by step throughout the process of reinventing yourself. Choose the right mentor: someone knowledgeable, experienced, and successful in the area you wish to pursue.

Ideally, this should be a person you can interact with directly, who will coach you when challenges arise and hold your hand throughout your journey of transformation. Mentorship does not have to be formal or paid.

You can approach a specific individual, share your intentions and explain why you chose them. Then, agree on a program or schedule to work with; even for free. Another form of mentorship is learning from a distance, where you follow and study someone without them even knowing it. This could be a manager of an organisation, pastor, motivational speaker, an author or even a top soccer player. You can also be mentored by multiple people, depending on what you need to learn from them. The key is to remain open, humble, and coachable.

10.   Network with the right people

Change the circle of people around you. Carefully assess whether they add value to your life, elevate your way of thinking, if they challenge your growth, and believe in your potential. Surround yourself with people who act as vehicles to carry you from a stagnant place to greater heights. These are the people who will help you rise from being shamed, looked down upon to becoming the most-read-about author, appearing on TV for the right reasons, or leading as a top employer, etc. But beware: death by association is real. If you remain tied to negative, toxic, or unmotivated individuals, their limitations will become your limitations. Their failures will bleed into your future, suffocating your potential before it ever blossoms. Associating with the wrong crowd can bury your dreams alive, keeping you trapped in cycles of shame, mediocrity, and regret.

Instead, connect with people who can transform your life to the glory of God; those who can take you from singing in the shower to performing on the world's biggest stages. Familiarize yourself with social networking platforms and use them wisely, not for idle scrolling, but as bridges to meaningful relationships that inspire growth, accountability, and destiny.

11. Follow up and stay in control

Megan stayed focused and committed to her transformation journey. From time to time, she reviewed her plan to identify if there were any deficiencies on her road map. Whenever deviations, setbacks or failures occurred, she changed the game plan but never abandoned the mission to attain her end goals. She didn't quit; she recalibrated. Megan mastered the art of resilience and kept grinding.

❖ Herald of Sunshine!

Today, Megan is a blessed married woman, with two brilliant children. She is a published author, international speaker, and licensed psychotherapist with her own practice. Who would have thought? She never succumbed to the pressure of her critics. She pressed on and never looked back. Now, she leads campaigns to help youth overcome brokenness, trauma, adolescent stages, women's rights violations and injustices that were designed to break them, suffocate them and sabotage their destiny.

She does not merely conduct couples and parenting seminars; she builds bridges across generations, stitching together broken bonds between parents and youth, and breathing life into families torn apart by silence and misunderstanding. Helping people is not just an interest; it is the heartbeat of her existence. She has walked through the fire of a brutal upbringing, scarred by rejection, crushed by abuse, violated by rape, dragged through the shadows of prostitution, burdened by teen pregnancy, suffocated by shame, condemned by society, and even haunted by the dark whispers of suicide. She has faced it all; every storm, every chain, every attempt to destroy her destiny. And yet, she overcame.

Where others would have grown bitter, she chose to become better. Where she was denied a helping hand, she became the hand that lifts others. Where she was abandoned, she became a shoulder to cry on. She transformed her pain into power, her scars into stories, and her brokenness into bridges for others to cross.

Now, she awakens the dreams buried deep inside those who have lost hope. She refuses to let anyone remain trapped in silence or suffocated by shame. Her life is living proof that survival is not the end; it is the beginning of a greater calling.

❖ Bearer of Dawn, Victory is Yours!

It's not over until God says it's over. No matter what you have done and what you have been through; your story is not finished. Kick out your dying blanket, shake off the dust of despair. Rise up and be counted amongst the living! Do not allow your past to bury you alive. Refuse to be chained by yesterday's mistakes, shame, or pain. You are more than your scars. You are more than your failures. You are destined for greatness. Reinvent yourself. Unleash the new you. Today, make a resolution to transform your life, to break the ground beneath stagnation, and to make things happen. Set principles that will anchor your soul, and live by them with unshakable conviction. Live boldly. Live purposefully. Live the life that God created you to live; a life of victory, of resilience, and of unstoppable power.

To all youth, while at it: *in all temptations let us consider not what he offers, but what we shall lose. "No temptation has overtaken you, except what is common to mankind. And God is faithful; he will not let you be tempted beyond what you can bear. But when you are tempted, he will also provide a way out so that you can endure it" (1 Corinthians 10:13).*

Chapter 12

Stand in the Gap

There are rare parents, those tireless souls who go door to door, seeking help, refusing to give up on their children. Even when every door slams shut, even when there is no breakthrough, they keep running in circles for their children, driven by love and hope. They are relentless, determined to support their children at all costs. They believe, against all odds, that there is some goodness left within their children, and with their encouragement, a positive turnaround is possible. But what does society do? It mocks them. Ridicules their efforts. It compares their children to others, as if pain were a competition.

My late grandmother, Mrs. Dinah Phuthi, affectionately known as Mmane Tina; once taught me something profound: *"Never turn a blind eye if you are in a position to help the situation. Do not laugh at another man's mishap.*

Life has a funny way of bringing you down from your high horse to cut you down to size."

Fair warning! Not every child will be like Megan, who managed to rediscover her purpose and transformed her life before it was too late. Not every child will be able to find strength to rise, find reasons to stay motivated, or the courage to hold on and not throw in the towel. The worst can happen. Your child could die, get arrested or contract incurable diseases. But today, thank God, you have been granted a second chance. You can still save your child. It is possible to mend what is broken. Yes, they may have hurt you. Yes, they may have disgraced you in the past. And yes, you are mad at them; so what? At the end of the day, they are still your children. Even if you turn your back on them, it still casts a shadow of that abandonment on you.

Have the heart to forgive. The world has forsaken them already. They face condemnations and persecutions from all directions. But you, as parents, must not abandon them as well. Show them love. Show them empathy. Tell them you forgive them. Help them weather this storm. Show them in an accurate and compassionate manner that you understand their experiences and feelings, or at least that you are trying to. And if you don't fully understand, that's okay. No one expects you to have it all figured out. Don't be too hard on yourself. Just be there for them. It's okay to admit that you're scared too, that you don't know how to fix it nor make it go away. Hold their hands. Seek help together, whether from a psychotherapist, a pastor or someone who has survived and came out whole from the same ordeal.

Each child's journey is personal, unique, and fragile; therefore, try to perceive things from the child's point of view. Do not be judgmental. Draw them close and encourage them to open up. Yes, along the way, there will be some resistance. Yes, there may be relapses. But do not be dismayed. It is all part of the healing and recovery process. Maintain the momentum alive in those purposeful conversations. Remember, the devil knows your prayer. He is pretty aware of the good plans you have for your children. He sees the greatness your children are destined for. So, he ruffles them a bit to stir confusion between you and your children, hoping to divide you. He is intentional. He knows of your little faith. So, he preys on your doubts, banking on you to give up, abandon and disown your children. But don't. God has already answered your prayers; stand firm in that promise. Keep on fighting for your children. Join in their struggles; together, you can conquer. There is nothing more powerful than a family that prays together. Stand firm! Hold each other's hands. Look the enemy in the eye; and refuse to let go.

Isaiah 40:29-31

He gives power to the weak and strength to the powerless. Even youths will become weak and tired, and young men will fall in exhaustion. But those who trust in the Lord will find new strength. They will soar high on wings like eagles. They will run and not grow weary. They will walk and not faint.

Chapter 13

Reposition Yourself

Parents, stand in the gap for your children...

When they are weak, be strong for them...

When they lose heart and relapses, stand in the gap and pray for them to regain strength...

When the world hates them, love them fiercely.

When the world attacks them, shield them...

When they see evil in them, declare the goodness of the Lord upon them, and remind them what God says about them.

Be the light of hope to them. Be their guiding voice of reason...

Speak life unto them, and they shall spring forth...

And when you grow weary and see no way forward, remember: My Jesus shall be the way, the truth and the life... From the beginning, He is the God who stands apart from nature and rules over it.

Conclusion

Parents need to be actively involved in their children's lives from inception. The upbringing phase of our children is not casual; it is foundational. It demands both parents to be mentally and emotionally stable, and it requires personal parenting readiness, parents who are intentional, and vigilant. This phase needs to be piloted with extreme cautiousness, sensitivity and open-mindedness. What you say or don't say to your child and what you do or fail to do for your child will be the determining factor of your child's destiny. Your success or failure as a parent will echo in the life of your child.

Disagreements between parents are inevitable, and they are allowed to voice their opinions. At times, it happen in front of the children. But when it happen, parents should strive to model healthy interactions with each other. Let your children witness maturity, not chaos. Let them see constructive dialogue, mutual respect, and emotional restraint. Disregarding and fighting irresponsibly in front of the children can easily threaten their security and stability. They tremble and their minds race with fears of divorce, broken homes, and a future in ruins.

Children must see more than conflict. It would be beneficial for children to observe the following after a conflict between their parents:

◉ Was there a valid reason that needed to be addressed, hence the conflict?

◉ Hear both parents' different points of view and their perceptions of the matter.

◎ Observe both parties' willingness to listen to each other and allow each party to state their case without interference.

◎ Were apologies exchanged, respect restored and reconciliation? These moments teach them that problems can be solved, that love can survive storms, and that family is not fragile; it is resilient.

◎ Was there a clear resolution? Was the outcome implemented? How has it improved the situation or benefited everyone?

We are raising future men and women of substance. Children need to see parents make up after a disagreement with a collective solution and mutual respect. Let them see that disagreements do not destroy families, but strengthen them when handled with wisdom. These good practices would allow children to comprehend that, there was a problem that instigated the conflict, and the problem has been treated as such and dealt with accordingly. The good thing about this is that for the children's *comfort*, it will let them rest in the assurance that their parents are not enemies; for their *serenity*, their family is still intact, and the children themselves do not *feel and blame themselves* for their parents' disagreements.

Stay Engaged

Honestly, it is of great importance to emphasise enough the need and benefits of parents' engagement in the lives of their children by intervening and offering them continuous personal support base at all times. It's vital to know what is happening around your children, and what they are exposed to. Do you know whom they are interacting with on a day-to-day basis? Be cautious about who else speaks into your children's lives. What am I saying? Parents often tend to look far, blaming external forces as the only bad influences on their children. Do not be deceived into thinking danger only lurks outside. Over the years, that perception has proven to be inaccurate. In some instances, it is an internal matter where you discover that the enemy is operating from within the family itself. The thing with family members, if not monitored and managed with clear boundaries, they can be detrimental. Yes, I'm talking about the uncle, your own brother who sells drugs, and their favourite flashy aunt, who surprisingly spoils them rotten with money. They do not work a day to save their lives, yet they always have money. Be cautious! They will flash money to entice your children and eventually lure them into their world. They will poison their young minds, convincing them that school is time derailing and mind-numbing. These influences are toxic. They glamourise shortcuts, undermine the value of education and hard work; making children believe that quick money is the answer. Before long, your child begins to echo the deadly mantra: "*Why work hard when I can make easy bucks?*"

Parenting can turn out to be so overwhelming at times. It baffles you. But when it gets to that point, do not retreat. Seek help. Parenting is an on-going process that we all learn and take each day as it comes. Besides, we deepen our understanding when we teach something to others. Your child is not only the infant that you gave birth to; it could be your niece, nephew, neighbour or your child's friend. They may be going through a rough patch, battling depression or worse suicidal thoughts. The signs are always there, and we choose to overlook them until it's too late.

You can save a soul. It doesn't have to involve monetary obligations. All it takes is caring, love and noting the sudden change of behaviour in other children around you.

A Salute to Parents

To every parent fighting for their child's liberation at all costs; salute! Yours is a daily struggle. Do not lose heart. Your children are your blessings, even when they offend you. God sees your tears and will reward your faithfulness. Trust Him with your children. He gave them to you, and when they are broken, depressed, terminally ill or prosecuted, get on your knees and return them to Him to fix them. He is still in the business of healing and mending broken hearts. God is able. Even when the world says your situation is beyond mending or is incurable; God says, "*I can.*" fix your eyes on God. He takes shattered pieces and reshapes them into something beautiful. And yes, He can. He is a Good God, almighty and merciful. He is able.

Life After Rehabilitation

Now that we've explored the depth of these insights conferred in this book, we now have to be attuned to move to the next phase: focusing mainly on life after rehabilitation. In most cases, the majority of the rehabilitees come from dysfunctional and underprivileged backgrounds; with limited resources, their wounds deep. However, that being the case, it's critical for the rehabilitees to embrace the fact that the universe has unleashed a new lease of life for them. In addition, they need to come to terms with the harsh reality of acknowledging that the journey ahead is not going to be an easy ride; but it is possible.

To maintain their sanity, they should learn certain maneuvering techniques to pick themselves up by any stretch, learn to navigate life with resilience. Their transformation is not going to happen overnight. They have to start somewhere and work with what they have to reinvent their lives, and that is where you and I come in. To ease adjustment, there are variety of support mechanisms that we can offer them after the rehabilitation. Evidently, the lack or little rehabilitation support system has been identified as one of the other factors that can easily cause a rehabilitee to relapse or live in isolation.

The society we live in today can be insensitive, condemning, and full of persecutions toward rehabilitees. I would like to bring it to your attention that the humanity and courtesy to forgive our reformed fellow brothers and sisters could be a first step to heal and define their social rehabilitation.

The End.

Reference

http://www.shegznstuff.com/blogofshegz/identifyingstrongholds

Deactivating the Code of